Endorsemen

Have you ever wished for the right book to deal with those hard issues no one wants to face? I found it when I sat down to read *Facing the Mirror*. Instead of suffering through life with issues continuously harassing us, Daphne helps us to look into the mirror of God's Truth and see ourselves the way He does. She says, *"Before you can ever truly reflect Christ toward others, you must first see Christ in you."* Get ready to be really changed from the inside out. This book and its accompanying workbook are powerful tools for personal or group study and for people of all ages.

—**Trina Hankins**, Mark Hankins Ministries

Daphne's writings are completely transformative, stemming from her own deep, personal journey of understanding God and His word. As a pastor and cofounder of international Bible colleges, I can joyfully testify that *Facing the Mirror* has revolutionized lives around the world. I am so thankful for this book, as well as the passion, consecration and love that flows from her life.

—**JudiJo Adams**, XPloreNations Bible
College + Russ Adams Ministries

FACING THE MIRROR

FACING THE MIRROR

Finding a Self to Live With

DAPHNE DELAY

Facing the Mirror: Finding a Self to Live With
Copyright © 2023 by Daphne Delay
ISBN 13 TP: 978-1-6675-0301-1
ISBN eBook: 978-1-6675-0302-8

Published by Harrison House Publishers
PO Box 310
Shippensburg, PA 17257
www.harrisonhouse.com

Table of Contents

INTRODUCTION

God Wants You to Know

In 1999, I was standing at the front of a stage in Ruidoso, New Mexico, after fearfully sharing my testimony with over 100 women. The Holy Spirit had prodded me before breakfast to spread the word for everyone to bring a mirror with them to the conference room. After speaking, I challenged the ladies to look in their mirrors and tell the girl looking back that they love her and forgive her. I had never given these instructions to such a large group before, and wasn't sure what to expect. But within minutes, the place began erupting with praise as one by one, women were healed and set free from the lies of the enemy.

In that moment, I stood in awe of what God was doing with the simple message of righteousness. The Holy Spirit whispered to me, "Write it down, and I'll put it in the hands of people you'll never meet."

I wish I could tell you I obeyed immediately, but I didn't. My first thought was, *Who would buy a book from a girl in Seminole?* Followed by, *I wouldn't know what to write.*

For the next 18 months, I ran from God's instruction. My mom and I attended many women's conferences together, and each time I was near a speaker's book table, my stomach would get butterflies, and I'd have to go back to my seat.

On a separate occasion, while at a pastor's conference with my husband, I visited the campus bookstore. The same butterflies flittered inside, but I pushed them away trying to make excuses for why I wasn't the right candidate for the job. The next speaker gave a powerful testimony of the miraculous ways God answered prayer and used people. At the end of his message, he had us stand to our feet and give God thanks for what He was doing in our lives.

As I lifted my heart and hands to Heaven and sincerely thanked God for salvation and the work He was doing in our church, He said to me, "If you won't do it, I'll find someone who will."

My heart was so convicted. I knew what He was referring to. I loved Jesus, and although I wasn't sure how He was going to use me, I repented for my selfishness and said yes.

Another 18 months passed before I completed my assignment and published, *Take a Closer Look*, in 2003. To my amazement, once I obeyed and began to write, God flooded my understanding with new revelation of His righteousness. Since then, I have been privileged to see God dramatically change lives through this message.

As I continued to speak, teach, and write on this topic—helping others discover the same truths I'd found—the Lord began prompting me to write what I thought would be an expanded version of my first book. I certainly had more stories, testimonies, and scripture to add, so I readily said yes this time. But in the end, what emerged was an entirely new book altogether. I believe, as with all good things from God, it was meant for such a time as this. Or should I say, it was meant for such a one as you!

God wants you to know how He sees you—versus how you've always seen yourself.

I have to add, writing this book was easy because I know God wants to use you just as He's used me. His righteousness has a purpose, and your understanding of it will open amazing doors!

Forever in His debt,

Daphne

CHAPTER ONE

Through the Fire and Past the Mirror

Love yourself, for if you don't how can you expect anybody else to love you?

-Author Unknown

What are people looking for? Really?

It seems there is something in every person's inner core, regardless of that person's background, that cries out for a standard, a set of guidelines they can believe in, adhere to, and find fulfillment through. It's what helps them stay focused and on the right course. It's what guides them back if they get lost. It's like the voice on their GPS that won't stop saying, "Turn around. Turn around. Turn around..." when we've missed the mark and find ourselves on a path we didn't intend to travel.

But what if you don't have that guidance system? Or what if it wasn't developed in you at an early age?

The Summer of 2010

I didn't understand why the officer said what he did, but I acknowledged it nonetheless. "Ma'am, your son is not dead."

This was the phone call parents dreaded. Our nineteen-year-old son, Benjamin, had left earlier that day to make the nine-hour drive back to Tulsa, where he was attending Bible school. He had been with us for Father's Day after a month-long trip to Alaska to help his best friends move their parents.

The three boys had invited another young man to move to Tulsa after graduating high school to live with them and get his feet wet in independence. Benjamin agreed to stay behind one day to help Cameron load his truck, and then the two would travel together while the brothers went on ahead the day before. Benjamin had made this trip many times and nothing seemed out of the ordinary as they pulled out with all of Cameron's belongings tied down in his old pickup, which was loaded to the gills.

Seven hours later, my cell phone rang. "Mrs. Delay, this is Officer Smith with the Oklahoma State Highway Patrol. Your son is not dead...." When the officer came to the hospital later to check on us, I finally understood why he worded his statement the way he did. In all his years in the highway patrol, he had never found survivors in an accident as horrific as the one Benjamin and Cameron experienced.

It's not clear if the boys dozed off, which seems unlikely since it was the middle of the day, or if the gravel on the side of the road caused their truck to pull to the left. Whatever the cause, in a fraction of a second, the driver's side door grazed a guardrail. At the normal highway speed of seventy miles an hour, it only took another fraction of a second for the guardrail to scrape all the way down the side of the pickup, pop the gas tank, catch the rim of the back tire, and flip them into mid-air, igniting the truck on fire.

The driver of a semi-truck behind the boys said he'd never seen anything like it. The pickup flipped only one and a half times, landing on its top, facing the opposite direction in the ditch on the other side of the road, fully engulfed in flames.

Cameron's elbow had smashed the driver's side window, giving him a way out. As he ran to Benjamin's side to open his door, the flames were already too hot to allow Cameron to reach him. Benjamin was in the truck locked upside-down in his seatbelt. Running back around to the broken window, Cameron found that Benjamin was now pulling himself out, and he helped him the rest of the way. Not knowing if the truck would explode, the two boys attempted to run from the increasing flames, but Benjamin collapsed ten feet from the pickup and had to be carried to safety.

Lying in the hot sun on the side of the highway awaiting emergency crews, it became apparent the boys were injured. Strangers had stopped to help shield them with blankets and their own shadows from the blistering sun. We wouldn't know the extent of their injuries until later that evening, but for sure, Cameron was bleeding and Benjamin's exposed feet, legs, arms, and face were burned.

A Defining Moment

Benjamin had always been a happy, witty child. In second grade, my husband was asked to be the senior pastor at a church in the small, west Texas town of Seminole. Although we moved midyear, it didn't take long for Benjamin to make friends at the church and on his summer baseball team.

Benjamin is our oldest child. There are six years between our two boys, and by Benjamin's ninth birthday, a little sister had also joined our family. A few months after the birth of our daughter and into the start of another school year, Benjamin began to withdraw and become uncharacteristically quiet. I suspected it had a little to do with the attention our two young toddlers received from everyone. They looked like their daddy with olive skin, and as with most children, they were just cute at that age.

Benjamin favored my side of the family with beautiful reddish-auburn hair and freckles. He was a handsome young man, but I recognized in him something I had wrestled with myself as a young girl. I didn't like looking different.

One night as I tucked him in bed, I questioned him about his unusual behavior. He was young and didn't know how to answer me, so I got him out of bed and stood him before the mirror over his desk. "What do you think about that boy?" I asked.

With a quick glance in the mirror, he closed his eyes and said, "I hate him. He's ugly."

No Matter Who You Are

Insecurity is an evil. It doesn't matter if you're young or old, male or female, American or European. Every human being has to come face-to-face with insecurity at some point in time. With the best of intentions, our friends and family can tell us how wonderful and loved we are, but unless we believe it for ourselves, insecurity has the ability to squelch dreams, mask truth, and redefine destinies. "For as he thinks in his heart, so is he" (Proverbs 23:7).

God has created every person to be unique, with individual gifts, talents, and callings. But with the world and media constantly blasting their idea of perfection on each new generation, it's

Life is a mirror and will reflect back to the thinker what he thinks into it.
-Earnest Holmes

hard to find your true self in the mix. From kids on the playground to executives in a boardroom, insecurities can arise from comparisons and a lack of inner confidence—and that's if you are close to perfect by the world's standards.

So what about the person who was abused or neglected as a child? How do the injured, the maimed, the rejected, and the self-inflicted find confidence in who they are in a world that barely lets the beautiful and perfect person survive?

Look in the Mirror

"Benjamin, that boy is not ugly. Look at him. Look in his eyes."

God had placed me in front of my mirror many years prior, and now the lesson that had redefined who I was would be the same lesson that would protect my son's destiny. Benjamin looked into the mirror again, and as he did, I said, "That little boy was created by God and is loved by Him and many others. He needs to know that you love him too. Look into his eyes, Benjamin. He's scared because he knows you don't love him. But God has a plan for that boy."

The Bible says, "Don't copy the behavior and customs of this world, but let God transform you into a new person by changing the way you think" (Romans 12:2, NLT).

Benjamin acknowledged what I said without saying a word but accepted a hug and a kiss on the forehead as I tucked him back into bed that night.

Over the next few weeks, I prayed, and our vibrant young son blossomed again as if nothing had ever happened. He continued through school, emerging as a leader in both his youth group and among his peers. Benjamin graduated with top honors and was a talented drummer with dreams of "saving the world" with his music and sheer enthusiasm. He chose to attend Rhema Bible Training College after high school, following in his dad's footsteps. (Benjamin was just five years old when his dad graduated from Rhema.)

Now ten years after that defining moment in front of his mirror, Benjamin was lying on the side of the road with third degree burns over more than one-third of his body.

Destinies Compete

As I stood by my son's bed in ICU, he was unrecognizable. Moments earlier, the nurse had shown us a colored diagram of the percentage of his burns. She said, "His age will help him. We add his age to his percentage of severe burns to determine his mortality rate." I thought, *Did I hear her right... mortality rate?* At my son's side, I could barely process this information.

I had stood by the bedside of many critical patients before. As pastors, my husband and I have been called in to pray with and encourage the faith of families in desperate situations. We have reminded loved ones of God's faithfulness to His Word and comforted families and individuals with hope and peace despite all odds. Many situations turned into triumphant testimonies, while some left us with nagging thoughts of "Why, God?" When there was no sure answer, in our pastoral role we would pray for "peace that passes understanding" (Philippians 4:7) for all involved.

But this time, I wasn't the pastor—I was the parent. More specifically, I was the mother. If I could believe for others but not for myself, wouldn't that make God's Word a lie? I couldn't allow my faith to change because it was now my son in the bed, no matter what it looked like. I wouldn't allow myself to entertain thoughts of death. Instead, my biggest fear in that moment was the nagging concern of what Benjamin would look like when he healed and how he would handle it.

There are only two options for a parent in this situation: have faith in God or carry a burden of worry and fear. I could only choose one; I could not do both. Thankfully, I had hidden God's Word in my heart (first for myself, and secondly for others), and it now brought great comfort to me. David was right when he said, "Unless Your law had been my delight, I would then have perished in my affliction" (Psalm 119:92).

We were told to expect Benjamin to be hospitalized for some time. He was on a ventilator to help repair the damage to his lungs and throat after breathing in the fire, and skin graft surgeries were a certainty. His burns covered multiple joint areas, which meant therapy and possible loss of mobility. As a talented drummer with a great future, this news was unacceptable— but we held to the fact that he was alive and we'd face tomorrow together, whatever it might bring.

Each night, my husband and I would be forced to leave the ICU and the comfort we found in being by our son's bedside, looking for any and all signs of improvement. As human as we were, we would look at each other and make the same statement night after night: "Tell me he's going to be okay."

Despite a swirl of emotions, I was reminded of Abraham's faith and how "contrary to hope, in hope [he] believed" (Romans 4:18). Now was my moment of truth. As any mother would, I cried as I looked at my broken child. Yet in that moment, I made a decision: I will not cry for tomorrow, for God's Word is true and His faithfulness shall be my strength.

The next day, I wrote in my journal:

I am fully convinced of God's Word. We will have victory in the midst of this trial. I have not lost heart because I am confident I will see the goodness of the Lord in the land of the living (Psalm 27:13). Just as Abraham chose not to rely only on natural hope (what you can do based on what others are saying), but instead chose to believe according to spiritual hope (what God can do based on what He has said)—I have chosen the same.

Seven weeks after the accident and six surgeries later, Benjamin was released from the hospital. He had endured a tracheotomy and many painful skin grafts. Because he had taken his shoes off in the pickup, his burns completely wrapped his right foot and lower leg to the knee. The flames on the passenger's side door had also engulfed his right hand, arm, and face. The left side of his body had severe second-degree burns, but none that needed grafting.

When we left the hospital, Benjamin's 6'4" frame carried only 132 pounds—twenty pounds lighter than before the accident. Most of his exposed skin was deep red and purplish in color, clinging to the fresh grafts. But his handsome red hair and confident wit soon took all onlookers past the scars.

Without a doubt, Benjamin's future—tough as it would be—was secure because he had learned at an early age about righteousness and who he was in God's eyes. He had discovered and developed a faith he could live by, a purpose he could live for, and a self he could live with—long before he found himself on a path he didn't intend to travel.

CHAPTER TWO

"You Be (Like) Jesus"

The art of pleasing is the art of deception.

-Luc de Clapiers

The Lord God said, "Let Us make man in Our image, according to Our likeness" (Genesis 1:26). So God created man and woman in His own image and placed them in a beautiful garden. But the serpent was more cunning than any other beast the Lord had made, and he tempted the woman to disobey God, thereby introducing sin. When the woman willfully disobeyed God's direction and then enticed her husband to do likewise, the eyes of both the man and the woman were opened, and they knew they were naked. So they sewed fig leaves together and made themselves clothing. When God discovered what they had done, He sacrificed one of the animals to make lasting clothes of skin for them, but as He presented the new clothing to the man and the woman, they said, "No Lord, we're not worthy. We'll keep our fig leaves." And they rejected that which the Lord God had done for them.

Okay, that last part doesn't exactly ring true compared to the Bible's account, but it is often true in real life, nonetheless.

Many Christians, although they've accepted Jesus as their Savior, are wearing layers of imaginary fig leaves because they don't feel worthy of His sacrifice. Like Adam and Eve, they began by covering their inadequacies with a small leaf, but quickly discovered it didn't hide their sins from God, so they moved on to bigger leaves. When their feelings of unworthiness were still exposed, it seemed only natural to dress themselves in something tougher—like the bark of a tree—expecting it to be more durable, protective, and harder to see through.

But the truth is, we don't need fig leaves, bark, or any other mask or covering to establish our self-worth. As Christians, our "life is **hidden** with Christ in God" (Colossians 3:3, emphasis added). Jesus is our covering. It doesn't matter who you are. If you struggle with regrets, failures, or low self-esteem, you are actually struggling with understanding (and receiving) the most beautiful gift God has ever given to man.

Adam and Eve didn't really reject what God had done for them, but we do know they were ashamed. Because of what they had done, they were embarrassed, humiliated, and most likely, in a state of disgrace as they put on the clothing God provided for them.

Centuries later, you and I aren't much different.

Daphne Didn't Like Daphne

I remember hearing a story about a mother and her two young boys who were in the kitchen one morning preparing breakfast.

As this mother poured the pancake batter, her sons began arguing over who was going to get the first pancake. Seeing an opportunity to teach them a lesson, she said, "You know, Jesus would let His brother have the first pancake." The boys immediately stopped arguing. Then, after a short pause, the older brother looked at the younger and said, "Okay, you be Jesus."

Cute story, but all too real for my comfort. Not because I had young boys who argued over pancakes (which I did), but because my entire life had been about trying to measure up to the expectations of others (you know, the "You be Jesus" part).

When I was much younger, my goal was to be popular—something I didn't feel came easy for me. In junior high, I ran for class president, won, and held the position through my senior year. Although I appeared to have some status among my peers, I later realized the leader in me was really just a follower. In other words, whatever pleased others is what I did. My heart had deeply-rooted insecurities. As a young person, when I looked in the mirror, I didn't see the same beauty

> *The greatest deception men suffer is from their own opinions.*
> *-Leonardo da Vinci*

I admired in all my friends. Psychologists would suggest it was because I didn't have a regular father figure in my life to tell me I was something special or beautiful. They may or may not be right, but I felt loved and accepted by my family. In fact, although my parents had divorced and remarried a couple of times, I don't remember ever feeling rejected by either of them. My granddad on my mother's side was always around and very supportive, and both my real dad and stepdad showed me great love.

So I would have to disagree with the psychologists. I'm sure my problem was that Daphne didn't like Daphne, and my eyes deceived me often. When I didn't see the same beauty in my mirror as magazines and television portrayed or peer pressure demanded, I fell into the traps of alcohol, drugs, and promiscuity, looking for acceptance. But these empty acts only increased the feelings of disapproval that welled up each time I stood before my pitiful reflection.

"You Be (Like) Jesus"

Through a series of events and very bad choices that landed me at the bottom of the bottom with nowhere to look but up, I found salvation at the age of 21. At first, I was elated. The love and peace I felt in the sanctuary of God's presence was unlike anything I had ever known before. But little by little, what I believed about myself before salvation soon overrode any and everything I was being told about Jesus and His love for me now. My deceived heart only heard, "You be (like) Jesus," which was something I definitely could not do.

I had well-kept secrets, and although I'd done a good job of hiding them from those around me, deep down I knew God was well aware of my past. So I believed if the goal was to be like Jesus, I had already blown that a million times over and nothing could change or reverse it.

Ironically, the same year I was saved, I met a young Christian man at the church I was attending, fell in love, became pregnant, and got married. Yes, in that order. I already wrestled with condemnation (what the dictionary would define as a self-pronounced sentence of guilt), and I now had one more thing to pile on my heap of disgrace. I couldn't even be a good Christian, much less be like Jesus.

Despite my struggles, God's Word became my lifeline to eternity. I clung to every promise of heaven hoping God would receive me someday. My goal was to survive until I would finally and forever be free from the condemnation that tainted everything about me.

Can you relate? You don't have to be a young, white woman, in middle-class America to struggle with these same issues. Guilt, regrets, insecurities, and condemnation are all weapons of Satan to destroy God's people (preferably before they come to Christ to keep them lost; but definitely after, to keep them from sharing their faith with others).

Satan's Best-Laid Plan Has Always Been for Us to Destroy Ourselves First

At any stage of life, Satan loves using the weaknesses of our flesh as a weapon against us; much like the bully who grabs our wrist, swinging it toward our face, yelling, "Quit hitting yourself! Quit hitting yourself!" Satan targets our insecurities and then laughs at our self-destruction. The Bible says we fall into his snare and are "taken captive by him to do his will" (2 Timothy 2:26).

By all appearances, I looked as though I had it all together after salvation. I wore my mask well, but my mirror remained an enemy. Every time I looked into it, I inevitably found something wrong. My husband and family assured me of their love, but I struggled receiving it because I didn't love myself. Don't get me wrong, I disliked the torture I felt on the inside, but not knowing how to end it, I simply prayed silent prayers for God's deliverance.

In my mind, an imaginary glass box imprisoned me. I could see through the top, bottom, and sides, peering out at all the perfect people in the world, yet it caged me nonetheless. As I viewed my world and those around me through the walls of this imaginary prison, I perceived that, unlike me, everyone else must have lived lives worthy of God's approval. There were times when I would forget or become numb to my feelings for a moment and then without notice—Bang!—I would hit the top of that see-through box and be put right back in my place, reminded of my guilt, shame, and regret for my sins. This mind-set confined me and limited my freedom.

In Romans 7:24, the Apostle Paul said, "O wretched man that I am! Who will deliver me from this body of death?" I could definitely relate to this statement. But Paul went on to say in verse 25, "I thank God—through Jesus Christ our Lord!" This part of his testimony I didn't understand. Was he talking about heaven? Or something else?

It didn't take long for God to answer my questions. And what happened next in my life changed everything.

The Mirror Doesn't Lie

It was like any other morning, except for one small detail. As I stood in front of my bathroom mirror preparing for the day, I heard a voice. I'm not sure if you would have heard it if you were with me that morning, but it was very clear to me. Although I was still far from being a mature Christian at the time, I knew it was God. He said, "Look closer."

As I looked into the mirror at my reflection, I expected to find something wrong (again). Was my hair out of place? Were my freckles uncovered? Is this blouse too tight?

But God said, "No. Look close. Look deep into your eyes."

As I moved closer to the mirror and looked into my own eyes, I looked at another person. The eyes in the mirror reflected a girl who knew my secret thoughts, fears, disappointments, hopes, and dreams. For years, I had attempted to hide her because she was the one guilty of all my mistakes. I had carefully hidden her away while I focused on the exterior part of myself that others saw. Yet as I stood there within an inch of the mirror, looking at nothing but those eyes—eyes reflecting great sorrow—God said, "Now, tell her you love her and you forgive her."

Standing face to face with my torturer, I was so surprised at who had held me captive all those years. I don't recall believing God was my torturer, but I did believe He was the One who held the key to my glass box (my imaginary prison). Trusting He knew best, I had accepted the imprisonment as an appropriate punishment for my failures. I could see God on the outside. I could see everyone, and I envied them. "Be grateful," I would tell myself. "God has allowed you to come this far; don't ask for more." And I never did.

Yet there I stood, facing my mirror with the answer to my silent prayer. The key had always been in my hand. The lock was inside. Whereas I had believed my sins were too great for God to pardon, I now had to face the realization it wasn't God who was withholding forgiveness. The make-believe prison was my own creation. Daphne couldn't forgive Daphne.

In One Sentence

Glued to the blue eyes looking back at me, I had flashbacks of horror stories I had heard about abused children locked in closets. The eyes in my mirror belonged to someone just like that, someone who'd been locked away, unloved, and unforgiven. Like the eyes of a child who didn't know what they'd done to deserve such treatment, the eyes in my mirror reflected fear, confusion, pain, and rejection.

Unable to look away, I cried a steady stream of tears for almost an hour as I tried to unlock my imaginary glass box and accept the truth.

"Tell her you love her and you forgive her."

In one sentence, God showed me that although I had accepted His Son as my Savior and received His promise for eternal life in heaven, I had never accepted His forgiveness for my sins. I didn't feel worthy of such forgiveness. Surely He knew all I had done. Didn't He know how many times I had failed? How could He forgive me? This kind of love and forgiveness was beyond my comprehension.

I had lived in a vacuum of comparison for so long, striving for the goal of perfection and approval.

"Tell her you love her and you forgive her."

I held the key.

In front of my mirror, God revealed His truth: "If anyone is in Christ Jesus, he is a new creation; old things have passed away; behold, all things have become new" (2 Corinthians 5:17). At salvation, I knew my heart was drastically changed, yet I was struggling between the old sinful person I was so ashamed of and the new person who was forgiven. Contrary to what my emotions and self-judgments were telling me, I had to free that hurting child in my mirror. So with forced effort and through sobbing tears, I looked closely into my own eyes and finally said those words: "I love you, and I forgive you."

In His wisdom, the Lord knew my guilt and shame were deep-rooted. Simply saying the words, "I love you and I forgive you," only scratched the surface. My problem had to be uprooted with sincerity. In other words, I had to mean what I said.

I remember that when I was a child, I had to pull weeds as part of my chores. Some weeds could be pulled up easily because they had very shallow roots. Others took a lot of pull and effort because they had deep roots. I soon learned weeds with roots left in the ground only grew back. That lesson served me well in front of my mirror. I don't know if another hour passed, but after more effort and many more tears, I yanked up the roots of condemnation and said again with more sincerity, "I love you, and I forgive you."

Finally, the door of my glass box swung open. Like the unloved child released from her dark closet, the girl in my mirror was freed from unforgiveness.

Forever Changed

Our eyes serve as windows to our soul, the real us. We look at our reflection in the mirror all the time, but we only see our exterior. Yet how we view ourselves has a greater impact on our lives than any other thing. Whereas we tend to look no further than the outside, God is able to look straight into our heart—into who we truly are. "As in water, face reflects face, so a man's heart reveals the man" (Proverbs 27:19).

I had been unable to see how my own insecurities, feelings of low self-worth, fears, failures, disappointments, and attempts to be someone I thought everyone wanted me to be, created the walls of my imaginary prison—my glass box. I built the walls out of a lack of knowledge of God's Word and His view of me. I didn't understand, much less comprehend, all I had received in Christ at salvation.

Tell her you love her and you forgive her. The voice may not have been audible, but those words forever changed my life. Little did I know at the time, but God's written Word would soon seal what He began that day in front of my mirror.

Your Turn

My son Benjamin was able to pull through a horrific event in his life because he had learned at an early age that God doesn't see things the same way we do. I was able to help him discover these truths because God so graciously revealed them to me despite my sinful past. The remainder of this book is designed to give you the same truths. I fully believe you will experience the same results, no matter who you are or what you've endured, if you'll set your heart to believe it.

CHAPTER THREE

Changing Clothes

One reason God created time was so there would be a place to bury the failures of the past.

-James Long

The Disney animated movie *Mulan*,[1] tells the story of a young girl who doesn't quite fit into her tradition-bound society. In attempts to bring honor to her family, she fails miserably. She tries to conform to handed-down traditions, but finds herself unable to fit into a mold made by others.

Embarrassed and ashamed, she hides from those who love her. While looking in a pool of water, she catches a glimpse of her own reflection and says to herself, "Who is that girl I see staring straight back at me? Why is my reflection someone I don't know? Somehow I cannot hide who I am, though I've tried. When will my reflection show who I am inside?"

Her father finally finds her, and, sensing her guilt and condemnation, he lovingly sits beside her under a flowering tree and says, "What beautiful blossoms we have this year. But look, this one's late. But I bet when it blooms, it will be the most beautiful of all."

I was definitely a late bloomer; and I'm not just referring to physical development. Even after God's amazing revelation in front of my mirror, I was still slow to grasp all that I had received in Christ. I couldn't deny (or explain) the weight that had been lifted off my shoulders that day, but because I am a creature of habit, I would always eventually find myself right back where I started—guilty, insecure, and ashamed.

The Holy Spirit began to regularly whisper a couple of scriptures to my heart. I'm sure I had heard these passages in a sermon at church, but I wasn't really familiar with them. However, each time I would make a mistake and sense an overwhelming feeling of guilt, the Holy Spirit would say, "There's no condemnation for those who are in Christ Jesus" (Romans 8:1), and then He would say, "You are the righteousness of God in Christ" (2 Corinthians 5:21).

I felt prompted to repeat these scriptures aloud to myself, and as I did, the guilt would diminish. For years, these confessions were my lifeline, but it wasn't until 1999, while leading a Bible Study at my church, that I discovered the definition of the big-sounding word the Holy Spirit continually whispered to me. In Beth Jones' workbook, *Getting a Grip on the Basics*,[2] she said, "Righteousness is right-standing with God and the ability to stand before Him without guilt or inferiority as if you had never sinned."

What?

By this time, I was a pastor's wife and a lover of God's Word. I had confessed, *"I am the righteousness of God in Christ"* for years, but never fully knew what it meant! I had seen the "big-sounding word" in my Bible and had guessed it meant to be okay with God—*but to stand before Him without guilt...?* No way! If I had known that was what I had been confessing, I would never have said it because it didn't describe how I viewed myself, despite the love and forgiveness God had revealed to me in front of my mirror.

Conforming to the Mold

The story of Mulan is about someone who doesn't understand who she truly is, like us Christians when we lack understanding about our righteousness in Christ—meaning what we've received through Jesus at salvation. If the reflection you see in the mirror is someone you don't know (or in some cases, don't like), that negative self-image will hinder your growth as a Christian and redefine your destiny. If you're a person who wrestles with regret, the result will be unnecessary condemnation. (Remember the self-pronounced sentence of guilt?) What you think about yourself affects everything you do, "For as he thinks in his heart, so is he" (Proverbs 27:3).

For the most part, we're all guilty of trying to fit into a mold. Everywhere we turn, the media and traditions of men try to conform us. We often give into the pressure because we want to be accepted and please others. It's human nature. But when it comes to spiritual things, it really doesn't matter who we are (young, old, educated, not educated, rich, poor, etc.)—each of us wrestles with feeling inferior to others in small or large ways. Some of us hide this well, while others obviously pull to the sidelines in fear and insecurity, allowing their feelings of low self-worth to dominate their lives. God instructs us to be humble, but He never intended for any of His children to feel inferior, much less unworthy of His approval.

Jesus died for all, and His righteousness was given for all.

Much like Mulan, who eventually discovered the truth of who she was and then lived it out despite all exterior influences, I had to do the same. My son had to do the same. Benjamin had to face the fact that he was going to carry the physical scars of his experience for the rest of his life—and be okay with that. Both of us had to face our mirror at some point or another and accept who we are in Christ. Forgiveness is required.

All men are not cast in the same mold.
-Author Unknown

The problem is that forgiveness is a funny thing. It's powerful enough to set you free, and yet it is often the one thing you withhold the longest. That was my problem. I knew there had to be more to my relationship with God than I was experiencing. It just never dawned on me that my growth was suffering because of the unforgiveness I harbored toward myself.

Punishment for the Crime

One thing I've learned is that Christians who struggle with forgiving themselves (for whatever reason) are tortured. Their lives are a vicious cycle of attempting to earn God's approval through their works, failing because the bar is set at perfection, feeling guilty for their failures and shortcomings, and then starting over again and getting the same results day after day, year after year. This inward agony can be compared to an ancient punishment for murder once used in third-world countries in which the murderer had the victim's dead body tied to his back. As the corpse began to rot and decay, the murderer would die a slow, painful death due to disease brought on by the rotting flesh. As horrific as this sounds, this is very similar to how Christians suffer when they struggle to forgive themselves. Their hearts have been made new through salvation, yet because they carry such deep regret, the dead man of sin is always tied to them.

Second Corinthians 5:17 says, "Therefore, if anyone is in Christ, he is a new creation; old things have passed away; behold, all things have become new." When I gave my heart to Jesus, I became new. The word "new" literally means new in kind, describing something that has never existed before. The term "old things" (also referred to as the "old man" or "old self") is a reference to our past life, which is marked by sin and separation from our Heavenly Father. In God's eyes, when we received Christ as our Savior, the old, guilty man of sin died—hence, the term "passed away." God never asked us to pick up the dead man, so why do so many of us insist on doing so?

When I gave my heart to God and became new in Christ, I couldn't seem to forgive the old me much less understand God's forgiveness, so I unknowingly created my own punishment. Like someone found guilty of a crime, I picked up the guilt, the shame, and the unworthiness associated with my old self and carried it around with me everywhere I went. Although I was born again, meaning I had given my heart to Jesus and became new on the inside, my mind and emotions constantly suffered a slow, painful demise from the guilt and shame I carried around. Just like was the case with me, this self-inflicted punishment is a major reason countless people struggle in their relationship with God.

You may be one of them.

Perhaps you've confused conviction and condemnation and therefore, don't realize the guilt you are carrying around is not from God and is only weighing you down unnecessarily. The Bible says, "God has passed over the sins that were previously committed" (Romans 3:25), meaning when you gave your heart to Jesus, God passed over all the sins of your former life as if they had never occurred. He forgave your sins and according to Hebrews 10:17, which says, "their sins and their lawless deeds I will remember no more," and He also forgot them.

Conviction Is How God Corrects Us.
Condemnation Is How the Devil Defeats Us.

If you don't know the difference between conviction and condemnation or if you can't accept these truths, your life and emotions probably look a lot like a gerbil on a wheel, spinning round and round between feelings of guilt and condemnation and attempts to be a better Christian.

Don't Run Around Naked

Ephesians 4:22-24 instructs us to "Put off, concerning your former conduct, the old man which grows corrupt according to the deceitful lusts, and be renewed in the spirit of your mind, and…put on the new man which was created according to God, in true righteousness and holiness." In this passage, we are told to "put off" our former conduct and "put on" the new nature given to us by Christ. Both require action.

For the most part, we know how to put off the old behavior. In other words, we have a good idea of what we shouldn't be doing anymore (Hint: no more lewd talk or inappropriate or immoral behavior, etc.). But because we are daily tempted by our old habits, what we really struggle with is how to put on (and wear) our new identity in Christ.

Before I learned who I was in Christ and how God saw me, my Christian walk revolved around trying *not* to do the things I had done in my past. I had a horrible potty-mouth! Without meaning to, I would cuss every time I got mad or frustrated. But what was worse was the guilt I felt afterward. I didn't have any idea how to put on and confidently become this "new person" the Bible talked about. I had a desire to leave my former conduct behind me, but I found it difficult. As a result, I constantly felt ashamed and inferior, not realizing that these were tools of the enemy to keep me quiet about my faith in Christ.

So, spiritually speaking, because I had put off the old man but not yet put on the new, I was running around naked! Now, how do naked people act? How would you and I act if we were literally sitting in a room together naked? We would be shifting in our seat attempting to cover ourselves, much like Adam and Eve were when they committed the first sin and realized they were naked. The Bible says they hid from God because of the shame of their nakedness.

The point I am trying to make is that when we only learn how to put off the old man (our old habits and sins), but never learn how to wear the new, we are spiritually naked. And naked people look for covering. Adam and Eve covered themselves with fig leaves because it was the closest thing they could find. Many times the closest thing a Christian can find to cover their nakedness is their old clothes—or we could say, their old behavior.

So the vicious cycle begins.

We have a desire to walk closer with God, so we put off the old man. But because we don't know how to put on the new man God created for us in true righteousness (versus false or self-righteousness, which we'll explore later), we find ourselves feeling naked, so to speak. We end up retreating to our old behavior because, according to our emotions, that's better than the feeling of being unclothed. But it doesn't take long before we feel guilty for caving in to the old man, so we throw him off again... repeating the cycle.

Eventually, if this process continues long enough, we stop putting off the old nature altogether and just carry it around in the form of masked guilt. This is exactly what the devil wants you and I to do. Remember, his best-laid plan is for us to defeat ourselves.

However, if you look closely you will see that there is a key to wearing our new identity instead of running around naked or staying stuck in the old. Look at our scripture again: "Put off, concerning your former conduct, the old man which grows corrupt according to the deceitful lusts, and be renewed in the spirit of your mind, and...put on the new man which was created according to God, in true righteousness and holiness."

The key is in renewing our minds.

Consider this: we put on a shirt one step at a time. First one arm, then another arm, and then over the head. In the same way, you can learn to wear your new identity in Christ by renewing your mind one step at a time through knowledge, confession and faith.

New Clothes

When God put me in front of my mirror, I received knowledge of His love and forgiveness. Then the Holy Spirit prompted me to confess God's Word every time I felt defeated. And finally, I came to a point where I believed God's Word, despite how I felt.

Knowledge. Confession. Faith.

These are the keys to renewing our mind and thus, wearing the new clothes God has provided for us. The Bible says, "I will greatly rejoice in the Lord, my soul shall be joyful in my God; For He has clothed me with the garments of salvation, He has covered me with the robe of righteousness" (Isaiah 61:10).

First, you have to learn the truth of your righteousness. Then you must build your belief system by agreeing with God's Word (learning to say what God says about you). And lastly, there must be a firmness of belief. These three keys are vital when it comes to growing and maturing as a believer. To break out of the vicious cycle of guilt, shame, and inferiority, you need to make a decision right now if you are going to believe God's Word—not just part of it, but all of it.

Hard-to-Grasp Truth

For example, you need to know God's Word regarding your right-standing in Christ because condemnation is a mean trick of the devil. He knows God is full of grace and mercy and will forgive your sins, so he lies to you and plants thoughts in your mind that are contrary to God's Word. These thoughts build up walls that keep the life God intended for you locked on the outside, out of your reach.

The mortar of these walls can be a combination of many things such as insecurities, failures, disappointments, and fears, all of which stem from your own inability to love, forgive and accept yourself as God does. Though you read about or hear great sermons about God's awesome forgiveness, each time you look in the mirror, your reflection will speak differently.

When I finally forgave myself, all 100-something pounds of guilt and condemnation (the equivalent of the "old me") dropped to the ground. I had become so accustomed to carrying guilt and shame around that I didn't realize the heaviness of it. Paul said, "Our old man was crucified with Him, that the body of sin might be done away with, that we should no longer be slaves of sin" (Romans 6:6). In other words, we don't have to be a slave to who we once were.

The hard-to-grasp truth for any of us is that our sins were crucified with Jesus. This means we don't have to be a slave to them anymore. But just like the convicted murderer in days of old, as long as you and I continue to hold on to the dead junk of our past, it will hinder where we go, what we do, and how we feel about ourselves.

Mulan asked a very good question, "When will my reflection show who I am inside?" I believe the answer is first found in understanding and accepting God's truth.

CHAPTER FOUR

Cricket Mentalities

I don't think of all the misery but of all the beauty that still remains.

-Anne Frank

Here's a statement that might make you think:

How we view ourselves will always have a greater impact on us than how we view God.

Think about it. How do you view God?

Now, in comparison, how do you view yourself?

More than likely, how you view yourself determines how you live your life. In other words, no matter what you've heard or read, or even positively believed about God, when you stand in front of your mirror, what you think about yourself has a greater impact on your life.

Children of God (or Grasshoppers?)

In the Book of Numbers, chapter 13, we find a good illustration of this tendency. God said to Moses, "Send men to spy out the land

43

of Canaan, which I am giving to the children of Israel" (verse 2). His directive was clear. God wanted tried-and-true leaders to spy out the land He would give them as an inheritance. He didn't ask Moses or the people to judge the land or its current inhabitants to see if they could or could not take it. His request for them to scout out the land was simply so they could see it for themselves.

Yet when the twelve spies returned from their mission, only two believed God's original word. The others all said, "There we saw the giants (the descendants of Anak...); and we were like grasshoppers in our own sight and so we were in their sight" (verse 33). Notice that how they viewed themselves overrode what God had said and promised to them.

The same is still true today. In fact, I dare say this story even gives us a good percentage of how many people wrestle with issues of self-worth: ten out of twelve. I believe it's entirely possible that more than 80 percent of the population struggles with insecurities, self-doubt, and inferiority issues. Now, how many of those are Christians—children of God?

The Bible contains numerous descriptions of God's love for us and how He sees us. I once heard someone say, "God's greatest joy is to be believed. His greatest pain is to be doubted." God desires for us to understand and accept His promises for ourselves, but sadly, just as God's children judged the promised land, many people judge the person they see reflected in their mirror based on how *they* feel and what *they* think, instead of what *God* has said. Instead of believing God's Word, they determine they are "like grasshoppers" in their own sight, and thus, must be in God's sight.

Kenneth E. Hagin once made this statement: "You see, a lot of times, our thinking is wrong. It's not in line with the Bible. And if our thinking is wrong, then our believing is going to be wrong. And if our believing is wrong, then our talking is going to be wrong. You've got to get all three of them—your thinking, your believing, and your speaking—synchronized with the Word of God."

This is so true of a large majority of the body of Christ. We don't realize our thinking isn't in line with God's Word. Jesus said it's not hard to determine what we believe: "For out of the abundance of the heart the mouth speaks" (Matthew 12:34). All we have to do is listen to what we say and we'll know what we believe. The spies revealed their belief system when they said, "We [are] like grasshoppers."

Wrong thinking leads to a wrong belief system; a wrong belief system leads to wrong speaking, and this is where we get in a mess. Jesus said if a man "believes that those things he says will be done, he will have whatever he says" (Mark 11:23). We prefer to look at this scripture in the positive, but it doesn't read "You'll have only the right and good things you believe and say." Unfortunately, it works in the negative as well. Every word we speak strengthens and empowers our belief system—right or wrong.

Sealed Fate

I once heard a story about a young boy who had caught a handful of crickets and put them in a wide-mouth jar. Inside the jar he placed your typical "cricket supplies" such as grass, flies, and berries. Then he put a lid on the jar with several holes punched in the top for air. Immediately, the crickets began jumping hysterically, trying to get out of the jar, only to hit the lid and bounce back down. This behavior went on for a couple of days and then suddenly stopped. Contrary to their previous behavior, the crickets became content within their jar, moving about inside it, eating and adapting to their new surroundings.

When the boy removed the lid, the crickets didn't notice. Curious to see what would happen, he left the lid off the jar but the crickets never tried to escape. Before, they had tried to get out, only to be beaten down. Now that they could leave, they contently stayed. Why? Because in the process of time, they had programmed themselves to believe their fate was sealed.

Many of us are like these crickets.

Proverbs 4:23 says, "Keep your heart with all diligence, for out of it spring the issues of life." In other words, be careful what you believe. If you believe you are a failure, an outcast, or unworthy, you will believe your jar is your fate, when in reality it is nothing but a barrier to the truth.

"Keep (or guard) your heart with all diligence, for **out of it** spring the issues of life" (emphasis added). Whatever belief system you put in your heart is what will come out. And whatever comes out of your heart is the picture you'll believe. For example, when the crickets no longer believed there was an escape, they stopped trying to find one.

In the same way, others can tell you the truth and even point to freedom, but if you don't believe it, you will never attempt it—no matter how good it sounds. I'll remind you again: "For as a man thinks in his heart, so is he" (Proverbs 23:7).

The Hebrew word for "issues" in Proverbs 4:23 is literally translated as boundaries or controlling factors. So the Psalmist is saying, "Keep (or guard) your heart with all diligence, for out it spring the [boundaries or controlling factors] of life." When someone beats us down with their words or treats us with contempt or prejudice, we tend to fight back, at first. But over time, the fight can get tiresome, and little by

It is what a man thinks of himself that really determines his fate.

-Henry David Thoreau

little, we begin to adjust our life to fit within the lie. The words and actions of others, and then our own words and actions, build an invisible prison.

Miserable and Lost

I have a friend who heads up a large ministry for people who struggle with sexual issues.[1] He is able to help these individuals because he, himself, came out of a homosexual lifestyle. When he was younger, some older boys in his neighborhood called him "fag" and other horrible names because he wasn't athletic or noticeably strong. Then, in a separate incident, he was molested by a boy in a pretend game of doctor. As the years passed, he wondered to himself if maybe he was gay. He didn't feel he was, but the words and actions of others had planted seeds in his heart.

When he entered college, he met some openly gay people and gravitated toward them, still wondering if this was his identity. Several years later, miserable and lost, he found his way to the ministry he now leads. The words and actions of others and then his own words and actions, built an invisible prison that not only confined him, but also *defined* him. After learning the truth and reversing what he'd believed about himself, my friend is now happily married and helping others find the truth of who they are in Christ according to God's Word.

But there are countless men and women today living in invisible prisons similar to my friend's or like my own glass box. Many were raised in Christian homes where they attended church regularly at an early age. Others, like me, did not begin having a relationship with God until they were adults. In either case, both can be programmed to believe God is unreachable and their sins are too great. The problem lies within. Their mindset is contrary to God's thoughts, and they simply lack knowledge of their identity in Christ. If asked to give a reason for their feelings, most of these strugglers would likely say, "I don't know why," while some might say, "Well, I've made a lot of mistakes." Both statements contain an element of truth and give an explanation for their struggle.

When someone says they don't know why they feel the way they do, they are simply admitting they don't have the answer. They really don't know. Now consider this. God said in Hosea 4:6, "My people are destroyed for lack of knowledge." Having a lack of knowledge is the same as not having the answer; the result is destruction. Similarly, when someone feels distant from God and believes his mistakes are the reason why, he is being destroyed by a lack of knowledge. He has allowed his understanding of sin to outweigh his understanding of God's love and forgiveness.

The biggest danger with either of these mindsets is that it is a playground for the enemy. In 2 Corinthians 2:11, the Bible says, "Lest Satan should take advantage of us; for we are not ignorant of his devices." Ignorance is not stupidity. The definition of ignorance is a lack of knowledge. This explains a lot.

God's people are destroyed because of ignorance; in that condition, Satan takes advantage of us.

We've all made mistakes, but it's the memory of them that often hinders us. God said, "Their sins and their lawless deeds I will remember no more" (Hebrews 10:17). Though God doesn't remember them, our enemy, the devil, wants to make sure we remember them. So, because our past failures and disappointments linger at the forefront of our minds, they compound with every subsequent mistake we make in our present life, causing us to feel continually unworthy of God's love and forgiveness. Our ignorance of the enemy's scheme causes us to adopt a failure mentality.

The Scale Is Tipped

Out of my ignorance and feelings of inferiority, I constantly asked God to forgive me of the same sins over and over. I was guilty of meditating on my past and the things I had done before salvation, never realizing I was only adding to the mortar of my invisible prison. My early years of Christianity consisted of a vicious cycle of wrong meditation and pitiful prayer.

In an effort to be freed from my feelings of condemnation, I kept continually asking God to forgive me of my previous sins, forgetting the truth, not believing it, or simply not fully realizing

He had already forgiven me when I received Jesus as my Lord. Because I thought Christians had to be perfect, my feelings of unworthiness were multiplied by my day-to-day failures.

Have you ever seen a balance scale? They are rarely found in use today, but a long time ago, they were frequently used in commerce and trade. For example, a gold miner would lay his treasure on one side of the scale while the banker laid the weights on the other side to determine the value of the miner's gold. The banker would put an equal amount of weight opposite the gold until the scale balanced.

I compare my early self to an unbalanced scale because on one side, I had a limited knowledge of my identity in Christ. The other side of the scale was weighed down with my full knowledge of sin. This lopsided understanding was the reason for the deception in my life and resulted in compounded guilt and condemnation and a belief that I would never be able to fully earn God's love.

Instead of feeling closer to God when I asked for His forgiveness for my sins and failures, I always felt more distanced and out of balance. But the Bible says, "The LORD is gracious and full of compassion" (Psalm 145:8). His desire is for every person to be saved and come to the knowledge of truth (1 Timothy 2:4). God doesn't just want us to be saved; He wants us to walk, live, and flourish in His love.

CHAPTER FIVE

The Truth About God

You can bend it and twist it... You can misuse and abuse it... But even God cannot change the Truth.

-Michael Levy

In the famous children's novel *Alice in Wonderland*, the Queen of Hearts is an interesting character. Overseeing the kingdom with the King of Hearts, she changes from pleasant to enraged every other minute. At the slightest offense, she shouts, "Off with their heads!" It seems ordering executions is one of her hobbies. However, as the story goes, very few were actually beheaded. The kind King of Hearts quietly pardoned many of his subjects while his foul-tempered wife wasn't looking.

King of Hearts

This story makes me wonder about how people see God. Do they view Him as a quick-to-judge King who enjoys shelling out punishment like the Queen of Hearts? Or do they see Him as the kind King of Hearts, pardoning the offenses of His subjects?

The Apostle Paul asked, "Don't you see how wonderfully kind, tolerant, and patient God is with you? Does this mean nothing to you? Can't you see that His kindness is intended to turn you from your sin" (Romans 2:4, NLT)? It's hard to determine exactly how people form their opinions of God. Maybe they had a hard father or a moody mother. In those cases, I could almost understand a misguided view of God since our earthly parents are sometimes the only example we have—right or wrong.

When I was growing up, I had a friend who was raised in a very strict Christian home. She often wanted to spend the night at my house because our rules were quite different and she could do what she wanted without consequence. Years later, when we were in college and I had become a Christian, we bumped into each other, and I was very excited to share my newfound faith with her. To my surprise, she had abandoned her beliefs. She explained that if God was as hard as her parents made Him out to be, she'd rather spend her life enjoying herself. I didn't know the harsh God she spoke of, so I left our conversation very sad.

The God I met and fell in love with was a King of Hearts. Despite all my failures and extreme sins, He pardoned me. The more realization I've had of how much He actually pardoned, the more I love Him and want to serve Him. The Bible says, "We, too, were foolish and disobedient. We were misled and became slaves to many lusts and pleasures. Our lives were full of evil and envy, and we hated each other. But when God our Savior revealed his kindness and love, he saved us, not because of the righteous things we had done, but because of His mercy" (Titus 3:3-5, NLT).

If I were to compare someone to the Queen of Hearts, it sure wouldn't be God. Despite all my mistakes, I've yet to hear Him say, "Off with her head!" Instead, His kindness has been generous and His love unfailing. This is why the Bible says, "God demonstrates His own love toward us, in that while we were still sinners, Christ died for us" (Romans 5:8). He is the King of Hearts and "with undeserved kindness, [He] declares that we [who put our trust in Him now] are righteous. He did this through Christ Jesus when He freed us from the penalty of our sins" (Romans 3:24, NLT, emphasis added).

We need to fully understand there was a penalty. But there was also a payment. When the order should have been, "Off with their heads!"—a new and superior order was made: "Restore them to Me!" The King spoke it and His Word was fulfilled, not because of anything we have or haven't done; His grace covers a multitude of sin. "[For if we are saved] through God's kindness,

> *Whenever you have truth it must be given with love, or the message and the messenger will be rejected.*
> *-Mahatma Gandhi*

then it is not by [our] good works. For in that case, God's grace would not be what it really is—free and undeserved" (Romans 11:6, NLT). The truth is, He is the King of kindness and for that reason, He has become the King of my heart.

God Is Love

First John 4:8 says, "God is love." This God who is love not only demonstrated His love by sending His Son to rescue us, but the Bible says He did it "while we were of no use whatsoever to him" (Romans 5:8, MSG). In other words, when we were offensive, repulsive, and full of error, God still demonstrated His love. "For God so loved the world that He gave His only begotten Son" (John 3:16).

I want you to think about that. Really consider it. God demonstrated His love for us—truly showed us who He is—by sending Jesus to die while we were up to our necks in sin. So why do some people (maybe even you) believe He is out to get us now? If God wanted to reject us, He could've done it before sending Jesus to die for our sins. But He didn't because He loves us.

So if God is love, what does He look like? One way to see God's true character is to substitute the word "love" with the word "God" in scripture. For example, the passages in 1 Corinthians 13:4-7, often known as the "Love Chapter," would read this way:

> [God] is patient and kind. [God] is not jealous or boastful or proud or rude. [God] does not demand [His] own way. [God] is not irritable, and keeps no record of being wronged. [God] does not rejoice about injustice but rejoices whenever the truth wins out. [God] never gives up, never loses faith, is always hopeful, and endures through every circumstance (NLT, substitutions mine).

These are the marks and attributes of our God. This is how He was toward us when we got saved, and it is how He still is toward us now!

He is patient and kind. He is not impatient or cruel when we mess up. He is not jealous or boastful or proud or rude, meaning

He is not jealous of "other gods" in our life (such as television, sports, or even our family). But He does love us with a jealous love because He wants to be number one in our lives. We can count on Him to be trusting, modest, humble and polite.

God doesn't demand His own way. He simply requests and then waits to see what we choose. He is not irritable, and He keeps no record of being wronged. Instead, He is tolerant, and He forgives and forgets.

The devil wants us to believe He is hard and demanding and apt to strike us with lightening if and when we make a mistake. But that's not the truth. Psalm 146:8 says, "The Lord opens the eyes of the blind; The Lord raises those who are bowed down; The Lord loves the righteous." To be bowed down is to be crouched in spirit—broken and hurting. "The righteous" is the term God uses for His children. What kind of Father would He be if He responded negatively to His children who were broken and hurting? Yet people everywhere have believed God despises them because of their sin. It is true that God hates wickedness, but He doesn't hate us. Even when we were trespassers before salvation, full of wickedness because our lives had not yet been redeemed, He demonstrated His love for us.

This is why God never gives up, never loses faith, and is always hopeful. In other words, He sees our potential. He saw it before we were saved, and He still sees it now.

He's a Good Father

Because of His love, God is called our Father. You may not have had an earthly father who demonstrated this kind of love, but don't let that be a reflection on your Heavenly Father. The devil is the one trying to keep you from drawing close to God by comparing Him to your earthly father. No matter how good your earthly father was or is, there's still no comparison!

"See what [an incredible] quality of love the Father has given (shown, bestowed on) us, that we should [be permitted to] be named and called and counted as the children of God! And so we are" (1 John 3:1, AMP). Jesus called God His Father because He was His Son. But Jesus also called Him Father because of His love. After His resurrection, Jesus told Mary Magdalene to tell everyone, "I am ascending to **My** Father and **your** Father, and to **My** God and **your** God" (John 20:17 emphasis added). Jesus wanted to make sure we knew we were included in the family. We could've been left as orphans, but instead we were adopted and brought into the family of God. This is why John said, "We love Him because He first loved us" (1 John 4:19).

He's a Good Shepherd

One day I was meditating on several passages of scripture that spoke of God being like a shepherd. As I did, the Holy Spirit gave me this short story:

> When the little lamb was born, it looked to its mother for nourishment and safety. The mother taught the little lamb how to graze and find food and water. As the lamb grew, it became more and more independent from its mother. Most of his days were spent with his head down grazing, and rarely did the little lamb look up. His mother had warned him of dangers that loomed near

the thicket, but the little lamb had never been face-to-face with real danger, so his mother's warnings seemed insignificant. Until one day...

The wolf eyed the little lamb from the edge of the forest. He noticed how independent he had become, and therefore, vulnerable. As the lamb slowly moved closer and closer to the edge of the thicket with his head down grazing on the lush grass, the wolf planned his attack.

Suddenly, the lamb was scooped up and hoisted into the air! Within seconds, the little lamb was in the embrace of the Shepherd and saved from ultimate destruction.

This is a beautiful comparison to my life, and probably yours. I was ignorant and unaware, but God was watching over me nonetheless. "For you were like sheep going astray, but have now returned to the Shepherd and Overseer of your souls" (1 Peter 2:25). For the most part, our parents or earthly caregivers did their best to nurture and keep us safe for a season, even warning us of looming danger. But in our ignorance, we kept our heads down, focused on our immediate needs and wants, oblivious of the presence of the wolf—or the Shepherd.

When my brother became a Christian, he excitedly tried to tell me about salvation, but I thought it was silliness. I was too consumed with my so-called life. But now I'm glad God was patient and merciful. In fact, I am in awe that He still stood by, ready and willing to rescue me even after I rejected Him.

Ignorance can be a killer. Some people are ignorant of God's love. Others are ignorant of His mercy. While others are just plain ignorant of His salvation, period.

Thankfully, the Shepherd and Overseer of our souls isn't offended easily. He is rejected every day, yet that doesn't stop Him from loving us. In fact, when God saw our condition, because He's a good Father and full of love and mercy, He made a plan of rescue. "This is what the Almighty Lord says: I will search for my sheep myself, and I will look after them. As a shepherd looks after his flock when he is with his scattered sheep, so I will look after my sheep. I will rescue them on a cloudy and gloomy day from every place where they have been scattered" (Ezekiel 34:11-12, GW).

One component of mercy is a desire to make things right. When our heads were down, God had mercy. When danger loomed nearby, God had mercy. When we should have been destroyed, God had mercy.

"Like a shepherd he takes care of his flock. He gathers the lambs in his arms. He carries them in his arms. He gently helps the sheep and their lambs" (Isaiah 40:11, GW). Sometimes children, who are naturally ignorant of the dangers of this world, lose their innocence at a young age simply because they weren't protected by their caregivers. Sometimes it is the caregivers themselves who inflict the pain on their young through direct contact or second-handedly because they are so consumed with their own pain that the young are left neglected, confused, and exposed to outside influences. This unfortunate cycle can continue for many generations.

But the Bible says God delivers us in His righteousness and causes us to escape (Psalm 71:2). I realize now God didn't just deliver and rescue me on the day I was saved. He also delivered me in front of my mirror; He rescued me as He opened up my understanding of His Word and as He revealed Himself in tangible ways. But the truth is, had I continued to believe He was hard and judgmental, I know I'd still be in bondage today, perfect prey for the wolf.

So whatever you have believed up until this point about God, I sincerely hope you are beginning to recognize how much He truly loves you. Your thinking may be small, but your God is big.

CHAPTER SIX

A Permanent Solution

The supreme happiness of life is the conviction that we are loved.

-*Victor Hugo*

In 1864, Abraham Lincoln wrote a letter to the widow Lydia Bixby in condolence for the loss of her five sons in battle.[1] Although the letter is now debated as a piece of literature, there is no argument as to whom and for what reason the letter was written.

Peter addressed his second letter in this manner: "To those who have obtained like precious faith with us by the righteousness of our God and Savior Jesus Christ" (2 Peter 1:1). Although this letter is read by many today, Peter was also writing to a specific group, for a specific reason. It seems he assumed Christians reading his letter understood and had faith in God's gift of righteousness to all believers. Yet, interestingly, many people today—to whom this timeless letter is still written—do not have faith in, much less understanding of, the righteousness to which he is referring.

The Bible says, "For He made Him who knew no sin to be sin for us, that we might become the righteousness of God in Him" (2 Corinthians 5:21). In other words, God made Jesus (who had never sinned) to become the carrier of sin for us (who were burdened with sin) so that we might become (upon accepting Him as our Savior) the righteousness of God in Him. This one scripture describes the great exchange Jesus did on our behalf. It means we literally traded places. For this reason, all references to whom we are in Christ are directly related to whom God has made us to be through the death and resurrection of His Son. In other words, Jesus became sin. We became righteous.

Our righteousness is both a position and a corresponding action. But before we get into all that, let's back up and look at how righteousness got its start. It will make more sense if we take a closer look at God's original plan for man.

Everything Began with Relationship

You know the story: Genesis explains how God created man for fellowship. Adam and Eve walked daily in the garden with God. They talked to Him, listened to Him, and simply spent time in His presence. They were close to God. In other words, they could reach Him. The Bible says God was very pleased with His creation of mankind.

The serpent, however, who was Satan himself, didn't like this relationship between man and God, so he plotted to deceive Adam and Eve into disobeying God by eating of the tree of knowledge of good and evil of which God had commanded them not to eat (Genesis 2:17). When they ate of the tree, sin (defined as disobedience to God's commands) entered the world for the very first time, and suddenly, the utopia of the Garden of Eden was lost.

> And they heard the sound of the Lord God walking in the garden in the cool of the day, and Adam and his wife hid themselves from the presence of the Lord God among the trees of the garden. Then the Lord God called to Adam and said to him, "Where are you?" So he said, "I heard Your voice in the garden, and I was afraid because I was naked; and I hid myself."
>
> Genesis 3:8-10

Adam and Eve were hiding in shame because that's what sin does. It causes us to withdraw from God. From that point on, because of sin and its consequences, mankind was separated from their creator. And without a plan to cover sin, man would never be able to reach God again.

Adam and Eve were very grieved by their sin. I dare say you can relate because most likely you've been grieved at one point or another by your mistakes. But Adam and Eve weren't the only ones heartbroken. God was also very saddened by this turn of events, but in His mercy, the Lord designed a plan to cleanse humans from their sins through the use of their most precious commodity: blood. Without it, none of us will live.

God made blood more precious than a substance that circulates in the human body to facilitate life. Hebrews 9:22 says, "According to the law of Moses, nearly everything was purified with blood. For without the shedding of blood, there is no for-giveness" (NLT). Leviticus 17:11 explains: "For the life of the body is in its blood. I [the Lord] have given you the blood on the altar to purify you, making you right with the Lord. It is the blood, given in exchange for a life, that makes purification pos-sible" (NLT, explanation added).

After the fall of Adam and Eve, God required the blood of bulls and goats to be offered to Him in order for sins to be washed from His sight. But there was still a problem. This didn't completely remedy the broken relationship between God and man—"for it is not possible for the blood of bulls and goats to take away sins" (Hebrews 10:4, NLT). Much like placing a rug over your stained carpet, the blood offering merely covered the sins. It temporarily hid them but was never a permanent solution.

But God had another plan at work. Back on that fateful day in the Garden of Eden, God said something interesting to Satan: "From now on, you and the woman will be enemies, as will your offspring and hers. You will strike his heel, but He will crush your head" (Genesis 3:15, TLB). This one statement gave a hint as to what to expect next. God had designed a temporary solution through the blood of bulls and goats, but His real and permanent plan of rescue would be through another means.

Fractured

When I was in the second grade, I stepped out into the street without looking and was hit by a car. Besides the sheer trauma of the event and some broken teeth, I also fractured my right ankle at the growth plate. A fracture is simply a break, or something left in a state of being broken. The doctors had to place a cast on my leg from my toes to my hip to make sure nothing moved while the bone healed. This was a long process which required me to be wheelchair-bound for almost a year. Thankfully today, both my legs are the same length, and I am strong, all because of the cast that was placed on my leg.

When sin entered the world, we were separated from God and our relationship was fractured. Yet the Bible speaks of how God reconciled the world to Himself. "For it pleased the Father that in Him all the fullness should dwell, and by Him to reconcile all things to Himself, by Him, whether things on earth or things in heaven, having made peace through the blood of His cross" (Colossians 1:19-20).

The word "reconcile" simply means to re-establish a fractured relationship. God's plan of reconciliation was for Jesus to be the cast, in order to heal what had been fractured. "But now in Christ Jesus you who once were far off (fractured) have been brought near (reconciled) by the blood of Christ" (Ephesians 2:13, emphasis added). The blood of Jesus became the permanent solution to man's separation problem, whereas the blood of bulls and goats had only been a band-aid.

I like the way the *New Living Translation* explains the reconciliation Jesus made for us:

So Christ has now become the High Priest over all the good things that have come. He has entered that greater, more perfect Tabernacle in heaven, which was not made by human hands and is not part of this created world. With his own blood—not the blood of goats and calves—he entered the Most Holy Place once for all time and secured our redemption forever. Under the old system, the blood of goats and bulls and the ashes of a heifer could cleanse people's bodies from ceremonial impurity. Just think how much more the blood of Christ will purify our consciences from sinful deeds so that we can worship the living God. For by the power of the eternal Spirit, Christ offered himself to God as a perfect sacrifice for our sins. That is why he is the one who mediates a new covenant between God and people, so that all who are called can receive the eternal inheritance God has promised them. For Christ died to set them free from the penalty of the sins they had committed under that first covenant.

Hebrews 9:11-15

What a plan! God is now able to receive us and forgive our sins because of the sacrifice made by Jesus. Therefore, He no longer sees us as sinners, beggars, or outcasts. When we accept Jesus as our Savior, God sees us through His blood. This is key because the Bible says God was pleased to offer forgiveness by the blood of Christ, "to demonstrate His righteousness" (Romans 3:25).

But that's not all. Have you ever been in a wrestling match where you or your opponent yelled "Uncle!" in order to be released? That's a good picture of how God reconciled us. We were held tight in the grip of sin as a pawn of Satan, but Jesus reconciled us back to God by making the devil yell "Uncle!" Satan had no intention of letting us go, but Jesus overpowered him. He did this by making peace through the blood of His cross. Peace is actually a synonym for the word "reconciliation;" Jesus made peace—meaning He reconciled God and man—through His blood sacrifice.

Be Aware of Satan's Devices

Be warned: Satan is still up to his old tricks. He will use anything he can to deceive us, including insecurities, feelings of low self-worth, fears, failures, regrets and disappointments. His goal is to separate us from walk-

> *No man was ever so deceived by another as by himself.*
> *-Fulke Greville*

ing in the fullness of God's plan. Remember, "Lest Satan should take advantage of us; ...we [should not be] ignorant of his devices" (2 Corinthians 2:11).

Satan knows how we see ourselves is a key element to our relationship with God. His goal is to get us to re-think whether we are truly worthy to walk closely with the God of the universe. Our struggles always boil down to how we view ourselves, because our self-image always has a greater impact on our lives than how we view God.

His Righteousness

So what is this righteousness God has supposedly established us in? In Chapter 3, we looked at Ephesians 4:24, where the Apostle Paul explained how the new man in Christ was "created according to God, in **true** righteousness and holiness" (emphasis added). I love this statement because it indicates this was God's idea. Righteousness (our right-standing with God) was never a plan devised by man; it was the forethought of our Heavenly Father. Psalm 11:7 says, "For the Lord is righteous, He loves righteousness; His countenance beholds the upright." In another place, the Bible says, "He shall judge the world in righteousness, and He shall administer judgment for the peoples in uprightness" (Psalm 9:8). No wonder King David prayed, "Lead me, O Lord, in Your righteousness" (Psalm 5:8).

It seems that just as 2+2 = 4, righteousness is the sum of God's desire and God's direction for our lives. If we will allow it to lead and direct us, then we can rest assured we are in the center of God's will. I believe this is what you and every other Christian desires. God never intended for any of us to live on a roller coaster of doubt and insecurity. Consider these words from the prophet Isaiah: "The voice of one crying in the wilderness: [saying] 'Prepare the way of the Lord; make straight in the desert a highway for our God. Every valley shall be exalted and every mountain and hill brought low; the crooked places shall be made straight and the rough places smooth" (Isaiah 40:3-4). Sounds like non-roller-coaster living to me!

Of course, we now understand Isaiah was speaking in these prophetic words of John the Baptist who became the voice crying out to prepare the way for Jesus. But what path was he speaking of? What task was laid out before Jesus? The Bible says Jesus would become sin, "that we might become the righteousness of God in Him" (2 Corinthians 5:21). John the Baptist was essentially declaring, "Prepare the way for righteousness!" And the result of this coming of righteousness? "Every valley shall be exalted and every mountain and hill brought low; the crooked places shall be made straight and the rough places smooth."

Watch Your Step

So the righteousness God created and prepared for mankind was brought through Jesus. The psalmist said of the coming Messiah, "Righteousness will go before Him, and shall make His footsteps our pathway" (Psalm 85:13). This is why Jesus declared, "I am the way" (John 14:6).

We could liken this picture to a minefield. If it were necessary for us to cross a certain plot of land to reach our destination, yet we knew the land was covered with deadly mines, it would be wise for us to follow the footsteps of one who had safely crossed to the other side. Righteousness has made His footsteps our pathway. The world can be a dangerous place, but we can safely maneuver through it by walking in the path of righteousness.

Purely by definition, righteousness is right-standing with God, including the ability to stand before Him without guilt or inferiority, as if you had never sinned. Righteousness was given to us at the new birth (when we were born again), and it continues with us as we continue with God. This is why the scripture says that if you confess your sins, He is faithful and just and will forgive you and cleanse you of all unrighteousness (1 John 1:9). God didn't provide righteousness for us just to watch us lose it the first time we fall into sin. But He also didn't provide it as an excuse or cover-up for us to continue to sin either. Righteousness was provided that we might be forgiven and cleansed from our sin, in order to bring us into the presence and fellowship of God. This was God's plan, and it is still His desire.

The conversations that take place in the book of Job between Job and his friends should remind us to take caution. Job became a little confused on the subject of righteousness, and his misunderstandings are written in God's Word as a warning and help to us. Job had been defending himself to his friends, some of whom had accused him of wrongdoing. After listening for some time to Job's rantings, his friend Elihu asked him, "Do you think this is right? Do you say 'My righteousness is more than God's?'" (Job 35:2). I don't think Job set out to be high-minded. He probably just slipped because of deception and ignorance. But if Job misunderstood God's righteousness, so can we.

If we'll follow the footsteps of Jesus, learning to stand in the presence of God without guilt and inferiority over our past or pride and high-mindedness because of our good works, our lives will be more than we ever imagined. God remains the same and His provision for us remains unchanged no matter how much time or what sort of circumstances come to pass.

Ultimately, Job's friend summed up his faith this way: "I will fetch my knowledge from afar; I will ascribe righteousness to my Maker" (Job 36:3). The word "ascribe" simply means to give credit to something or someone. Elihu understood the provision of righteousness comes by God alone, its originator, and should be received by us, its beneficiaries, gratefully. It's an indescribable gift with amazing benefits.

CHAPTER SEVEN

The Free Gift

God's gifts put man's best dreams to shame.
-Elizabeth Barret Browning

Have you ever received a gift that was hard to accept? One that was really over-the-top, something you felt you did not deserve? I have, on many occasions actually. It's a two-fold issue for me. First, I have a strong work ethic, so I often feel I can only receive things I have worked hard for. But second, I struggle with not feeling worthy of generosity.

One time in particular, I remember receiving a gift from a friend of mine who was always quite generous. She often bought me things as random acts of kindness. I was a young mom, and money was very tight in our home. She was single and a career woman with extra to spend. I didn't realize how much I struggled with receiving until one day she said to me, "Don't rob me of a blessing!"

Her words have stuck with me to this day, especially now that I'm able to be the giver. There is such joy in being able to bless others for no particular reason, other than just because you can and it was on your heart to do so.

God feels the same way.

We know God is a giver. "For God so loved the world that He **gave** His only begotten Son, that whoever believes in Him should not perish but have everlasting life" (John 3:16, emphasis added). First and foremost, He gave His Son, His very best. Yet people everywhere struggle with receiving this gift of life. Because we are in desperate need of a Savior, many of us accept salvation, but only on conditions we can come to terms with. For example, we'll receive the promise of eternal life and a home in heaven. To a point, we'll even receive forgiveness of sins, but only enough to get us saved. We wrestle with accepting anything more than that because we feel undeserving.

Learning to Accept His Gift

This was exactly my problem. I had come to a point where I knew I couldn't continue in this life on my own. I believed and was convinced I needed Jesus as my Savior, so if receiving forgiveness of sins was what it took for me to receive eternal life, then I would accept it—to a point. But then my strong work ethic quickly kicked in, causing me to feel I must *earn* my salvation. This soon became a stumbling block in my life. The more I learned about God's love and acceptance, the more I struggled with feeling unworthy of His generosity.

In many ways, I could relate more to Adam than to Jesus. The Bible says, "Therefore, as sin came into the world through one man (Adam), and death as a result of sin, so death spread to all men, [no one being able to stop it or to escape its power] because all men sinned" (Romans 5:12, AMP, explanation added). One thing was for sure, I didn't need to be convinced I was a sinner. This I knew all too well. I was always aware of my sin. "For I acknowledge my transgressions, and my sin is always before me" (Psalm 51:3).

After being born again with the promise of eternal life, I still struggled because I identified more with Adam's sin than with the righteousness Christ imparted to me. What I didn't understand was that God had given me a gift. As with so many other gifts I had received in my life, I was rejecting it, not feeling worthy or deserving of it.

The sin that spread from Adam to mankind is anything but a gift! It is an inherent nature, meaning we are born with it. It isn't a matter of receiving it or not, it is just something every person has from the moment of conception. But what Jesus offers to those who believe is a true gift, meaning we are given a choice whether or not to receive it. His gift is righteousness. "For if by the one man's offense death reigned through the one, much more those who receive abundance of grace and of the gift of righteousness will reign in life through the One, Jesus Christ" (Romans 5:17, emphasis added). The New Living translation says, "...for all who receive it (this gift) will live in triumph over sin and death..." (explanation added). In other words, Jesus wasn't just giving us forgiveness of sins and an identity in Him, He was also giving us the ability to triumph over our circumstances through His authority. This is what it means to reign in life! So this gift of righteousness truly encompasses everything the believer needs!

Abounded to Many

Surprisingly, the gift of righteousness that was given through Jesus and the offense of sin that was given through Adam have an important similarity. The Bible says they both "abounded to many."

We know sin abounded to everyone, from Adam's first child to now. But once Jesus reconciled Himself to the world through the blood of His cross and His resurrection from the dead, righteousness also abounded! That's where the commonality stops. **"The free gift is not like the offense.** For if by the one man's offense many died, much more the grace of God and the gift of grace of the one Man, Jesus Christ, abounded to many. And the gift is not like that which came through the one who sinned. For the judgment which came from one offense resulted in condemnation, but the free gift which came from many offenses resulted in justification" (Romans 5:15-16, emphasis added).

Did you catch that? One resulted in condemnation (judgment, disapproval, criticism, dishonor, disgrace, and contempt). The other resulted in justification (approval, blessing, esteem, acceptance, regard, and respect). No wonder we have struggled with receiving this magnificent gift! The first set of words is easy to identify with; the second set contains words we would use when describing our admiration for Christ—not ourselves.

Another important word associated with the righteousness we've received is *favor*. Interestingly, this word is often used to describe a token or gift given to attendees at a party. The guests aren't the ones being celebrated, yet they receive a party favor nonetheless. Or maybe I should say they are offered a party favor.

As Christians, we understand Jesus is the one whom we love and celebrate. Yet, He offers all who come to Him something extraordinary, His favor (His gift of righteousness).

Righteous Favor

In the Scriptures, we find God showing special favor to many individuals. One particular recipient of His favor is the special woman chosen to bring Jesus into this world. It seems the only time we speak of the Virgin Mary or gravitate toward her story is during the Christmas holidays, but I have found great revelation through her account, regardless of the time of year.

We would all agree she is definitely one who found favor with God. In fact, the angel Gabriel said to her, "Rejoice, highly favored one, the Lord is with you; blessed are you among women!" (Luke 1:28). I'm sure Mary was quite taken aback that an angel was in her room, much less talking to her. But the scriptures say it was his words that troubled her the most. "When she saw him, she was troubled **at his saying,** and considered what manner of greeting this was. Then the angel said to her, 'Do not be afraid, Mary, for you have found favor with God'" (Luke 1:29-30, emphasis added).

The word "favor" is translated in other places in Scripture as acceptance, kindness, great respect, to be loved by another, or to be pleased with. We see the same spoken over Daniel, Jesus, Esther, Ruth, David, and many others—and rightly so. From our perspective and vantage point, they all did great things for God and, therefore, were deserving of God's favor.

In the dictionary, you will find that favor also means:

1. Something done or granted out of goodwill, rather than from justice; a kindly act.
2. The state of being approved or held in regard.
3. Excessive kindness or unfair partiality; preferential treatment.
4. A gift bestowed as a token of goodwill, kind regard, love, etc.[1]

Without a doubt, Mary must have been something special—but she couldn't have been without sin.

Romans 3:23 states that all people have sinned; they have all fallen short of God's glory. Remember through Adam, sin entered the world and spread to all men, causing all to sin. There was only one who was not affected by the fall of Adam. "We have a chief priest who is able to sympathize with our weaknesses. He was tempted in every way that we are, but he (alone) didn't sin" (Hebrews 4:15, GW, explanation added). So as lovely and chaste as Mary was, she couldn't have been sinless because only our Savior was sinless. This fact should encourage us because the Bible says despite everyone's propensity to sin, "His favor is with everyone who has an undying love for our Lord Jesus Christ" (Ephesians 6:24, GW).

So what does this mean for us?

Favor means acceptance: "To the praise of the glory of His grace, wherein He has made us accepted in the Beloved" (Ephesians 1:6).

Favor means great respect and kindness: "When God our Savior made his kindness and love for humanity appear, he saved us, but not because of anything we had done to gain His approval. Instead, because of his mercy he saved us through the washing in which the Holy Spirit gives us new birth and renewal" (Titus 3:4-5. GW).

Favor means to be loved: "But God is rich in mercy because of his great love for us. We were dead because of our failures, but he made us alive together with Christ. (It is God's kind-ness that saved you.) God has brought us back to life together with Christ Jesus and has given us a position in heaven with him" (Ephesians 2:4-6, GW).

You can give without loving, but you can never love without giving.
-Victor Hugo

Just as God looked upon Mary favorably, He looks upon you and me the same way. You might be tempted to say, "But Mary was a virgin. She didn't have the past I have." This may be true, but virginity is more than just being an unmarried, untouched woman; it is a state of purity, a state of holiness. God's Word says, "But you have been washed and made holy, and you have received God's approval in the name of the Lord Jesus Christ and in the Spirit of our God" (1 Corinthians 6:11, GW).

Regardless of your past, you were made pure and holy and righteous in His sight the moment you confessed and believed upon Jesus Christ as your Savior. "For if by the one man's offense death reigned through the one, much more those who receive abundance of grace and of the gift of righteousness will reign in life through the One, Jesus Christ. Therefore, as through one man's offense judgment came to all men, result-ing in condemnation, even so through one Man's righteous act the free gift came to all men, resulting in justification of life" (Romans 5:17-18, emphasis added).

It's hard to receive such grace and favor, especially in the form of a gift. But just as the angel said to Mary, the Lord would say to us, "Don't be afraid (overwhelmed, worried, fearful, or condemned)… You have found favor (acceptance and great respect) with God. He is pleased with you and you are loved by Him."

Oh, Happy Day!

As an illustration, I want to share a story with you. In 2004, all 276 members of Oprah's studio audience experienced a surreal moment. Every person, whether related or not, received keys to a brand-new car.[2] This was an unheard of present for that many people at one time. Reporters said the place erupted as people yelled, cried, screamed, sat down in disbelief, or jumped for joy! They were in awe of the magnitude of the gift they had received. I'm sure in some form or another they said, "Oh happy day!"

Prior to this give-away, Oprah had instructed her staff to find those who were deserving, meaning they had to find people who were in desperate need of a car. Her staff reported back that only 57 people were found, a number far less than what her studio would hold. So Oprah agreed to go ahead with the give-away to the entire studio audience, whether they all met the requirements or not.

Colossians 1:12 says we should give "thanks to the Father who has qualified us to be partakers of the inheritance of the saints in the light." To qualify for something means you meet the proper or necessary characteristics or requirements. We could say you are deserving. But concerning salvation and righteousness, you and I did not meet the qualifications (not even close!), so we had to be qualified by some other means.

Remember, God's desire was to restore mankind. When we were buried under the heavy weight of sin with no means to help ourselves, God, with great generosity, gave His Son to the world as the perfect offering, the perfect gift. "For by the power of the eternal Spirit, Christ offered himself to God as a perfect sacrifice for our sins. That is why he is the one who mediates the new covenant between God and people, so that all who are invited can receive the eternal inheritance God has promised to them. For Christ died to set them free from the penalty of the sins they had committed" (Hebrews 9:14b-15, NLT).

Can you picture a studio audience who has just been told that under their chairs is a box holding the keys to forgiveness and eternal life? At the revelation that they have been freed from the punishment of their sins, the place would erupt (wouldn't it?)! In disbelief, some might yell in exuberant joy, while others might simply weep at the thought. Others might sit down in awe of what they've received, attempting to understand it all, while still others might rejoice like winners after the greatest victory of all time.

Oh, happy day! Hebrews 9:12 says Christ "...entered the Most Holy Place once for all, having obtained eternal redemption." Eternal redemption means permanent deliverance. I like the wording "once for all." Jesus will not have to die a second time. He went to the cross *once*. And He did it for *all*.

Deserving or not, He "qualified us to be partakers of the inheritance of the saints in the light." He made us fit to receive and take part in everything God has for us. So forget the car. Forget the party favors. There is nothing that can compare to the gift of eternal redemption, our gift of righteousness. Nothing. In light of the revelation of this great gift, everything else fades in comparison.

CHAPTER EIGHT

Qualified and Convinced

To forgive is to set a prisoner free, and then discover the prisoner was you.

-Lewis B. Smedes

I recently went to an amusement park with several friends and our children. When one of the braver kids realized you had to be a certain height to ride, he became nervous he wouldn't meet the standard. Thankfully, he was a couple of inches taller than the height requirement, so it wasn't a problem. But have you ever seen a child walk up to an amusement ride only to discover they are short of the required height to get on? Even if they try to stretch and tippy-toe themselves a little higher, the standard is set, and they are disqualified (for now).

The Bible says, "For all have sinned and **fall short** of the glory of God" (Romans 3:23, emphasis added). The *New Living Translation* says, "For everyone has sinned; all fall short of God's glorious standard." Sin is universal. All have fallen short of the standard set for God's glory. But just like the child who grew an inch over the summer and didn't have a problem being tall enough to ride the ride on his next visit to the amusement park, we, too, have been raised up.

The standard didn't change. We did.

Not Short of the Glory

In his letter to the Romans, the Apostle Paul explains that everyone must meet the standard—no matter who you are or what you've done (Romans 3:21-24). But the good news is the standard is met through faith in Jesus Christ. God made it possible for all who believe to be declared not guilty or disqualified. This means you're not short of the glory any longer!

You and I have been justified by our faith in Jesus. "Moreover whom He predestined, these He also called; whom He called, these He also justified; and whom He justified, these He also glorified" (Romans 8:30). This passage isn't insinuating God has favorites. On the contrary, it is identifying how God made it possible for us to be raised up. "God knew what he was doing from the very beginning. He decided from the outset to shape the lives of those who love him along the same lines as the life of his Son. The Son stands first in the line of humanity he restored. We see the original and intended shape of our lives there in him. After God made that decision of what his children should be like, he followed it up by calling people by name. After he called them by name, he set them on a solid basis with himself. And then, after getting them established, he stayed with them to the end, gloriously completing what he had begun" (Romans 8:29-30, MSG).

Every person has fallen short, but God has provided a spiritual resurrection for those in Christ. "Because of His great love with which He loved us, even when we were dead in trespasses, made us alive together with Christ (by grace you have been saved), and raised us up together, and made us sit together in the heavenly places in Christ Jesus" (Ephesians 2:4-6).

Earlier, I compared our spiritual raising to a child who grew over the summer in order to be qualified to ride the rides, but that's not an entirely accurate picture. In the natural, a child at the amusement park who finds they are short of the height standard can only wait and *hope* they will grow taller in order to be qualified next time. But spiritually-speaking, when you gave your heart and life to Jesus through salvation, God *instantly* raised you up.

Although you were once disqualified from God's glory because of sin, your faith in Christ raised you to His standard! It's as if Jesus was the conductor at the amusement ride, and when you approached Him and found yourself short of the standard, instead of rejecting and turning you away, Jesus picked you up and put you on His shoulders, giving you joint seating with Him.

Raised Up

"Sitting together in heavenly places in Christ Jesus" does not only refer to a future position you will have in heaven; it also describes what you have now. Eternal life is not just a span of time in which you will live someday; it is also a quality of life that begins the moment you give your heart and life to Jesus

Christ. You were "raised with Him through faith in the working of God, who raised Him (Jesus) from the dead" (Colossians 2:12, explanation added). This is present tense, not future tense.

Nothing is more wretched than the mind of a man conscious of guilt.
-Maccius Plautus

The Bible doesn't say we will be raised; it says we were raised. "And you, being dead in your trespasses and the uncircumcision of your flesh, He has made alive together with Him, having forgiven you all trespasses, having wiped out the handwriting of requirements that was against us, which was contrary to us. And He has taken it out of the way, having nailed it to the cross" (Colossians 2:13-14).

Can you imagine the delight of the disqualified child who, when the conductor removed the measuring stick, was suddenly qualified by grace? The child knows it wasn't his or her own doing; it was by grace and grace alone. They were short of the standard (the glory of God), yet the scripture says, "Whoever believes on Him will not be put to shame" (Romans 10:11). This is true for every person, no matter who they are or what they've done.

I was like that child, except I held my own measuring stick. Before I even approached, I mentally disqualified myself. It was torturous to watch everyone else enjoy the ride, while I stood off to the side. Very timidly, little by little, I approached the throne of grace and was delighted when I discovered God had His own measuring stick, and it was nothing like mine! "But to each one of us grace was given according to the measure of Christ's gift" (Ephesians 4:7). God didn't measure me according to my standard (good, bad, or ugly); He measured me according to Christ's gift.

The Requirement Was Fulfilled

But that's not all. Paul said those who are in Christ Jesus, who walk and live their lives according to the Spirit, are not under the law of condemnation, for they have been raised up. "For the law of the Spirit of life in Christ Jesus has made me free from the law of sin and death. For what the law could not do in that it was weak through the flesh, God did by sending His own Son in the likeness of sinful flesh, on account of sin: He condemned sin in the flesh, that the righteous requirement of the law might be fulfilled in us who do not walk according to the flesh but according to the Spirit" (Romans 8:2-4). God sent His Son Jesus to set us free from sin and death. On our own, you and I could never pay the price needed to be reconciled with God. But Jesus became our substitution and paid the penalty for our sins "that the righteous requirement of the law might be fulfilled."

What is the "righteous requirement" Paul is speaking of? The answer is found in 2 Corinthians 5:21: "For He made Him who knew no sin to be sin for us, that we might become the **righteousness** of God in Him" (emphasis added). Righteousness is a big-sounding word, but we've learned it means to have right-standing with God. More specifically, it includes the ability to stand before Him without any guilt or inferiority as if you had never sinned.

Given this expanded definition, most Christians wouldn't say this describes their relationship with God. Most will agree we have a sin nature and we've all blown it. We're thankful for God's forgiveness, and we're thankful for our salvation and the promise to live eternally in heaven. But to daily feel like we can stand before God guilt-free? No way!

Yet the scripture clearly says, "For He (God) made Him (Jesus) who knew no sin (who was perfect, who had never sinned) to be sin for us (who were not perfect and guilty of sin), that we might become (upon accepting Jesus as our Lord) the righteousness of God in Him (right-standing with God and the ability to stand before Him without any guilt or inferiority as if we had never sinned)" (my paraphrase).

This was the "righteous requirement" Paul was referring to in his letter to the Romans. This isn't my opinion. This is what the Bible says. So if Jesus paid the penalty for our sins so we could receive His righteousness, isn't it important for us to better understand what righteousness is and how we receive it?

Accounted for Righteousness

The first mention of righteousness is found in Genesis 15:5, when God made a promise to Abraham. He said, "Look now toward heaven, and count the stars if you are able to number them… So shall your descendants be." This was quite a promise. If you've ever studied the stars on a clear night, there are too many to count. Yet Abraham responded in faith. "He [Abraham] believed in the Lord, and He [God] accounted it to him for righteousness" (Genesis 15:6, explanation added). At the time of this promise, Abraham had no children of his own, but God said his descendants would be as many as the number of stars in the sky. Without questioning why or how this could happen, Abraham simply believed God.

The New Testament describes this exchange between God and Abraham as a promise, or covenant. "For when God made a promise to Abraham, because He could swear by no one greater, He swore by Himself, saying, 'Surely blessing I will bless you, and multiplying I will multiply you.' And so, after [Abraham] had patiently endured, he obtained the promise" (Hebrews 6:13-15, explanation added). By definition, a covenant is a contract or agreement between two parties, where each party offers its best to the other. Our God is perfect, so it is impossible for Him to lie (Hebrews 6:18). Abraham was a mere man, like you and I, having faults and a sin nature. Therefore, how could God, being perfect, actually make covenant with an imperfect man? He couldn't. So He made a covenant with Himself on Abraham's behalf.

But that's not all. God, as the creator of the universe, had everything to offer Abraham in this covenant. But what did Abraham have to give?

Look at Genesis 15:5-6 again: "Then He brought him outside and said, 'Look now toward heaven, and count the stars if you are able to number them.' And He said to him, 'So shall your descendants be.' And he [Abraham] **believed** in the Lord, and He accounted it to him for righteousness" (emphasis added). God could literally offer everything to Abraham, and in exchange, all He wanted was to be believed.

The Bible says, "He [Abraham] did not waver at the promise of God through unbelief, but was strengthened in faith, giving glory to God, and being fully convinced that what He had promised He was also able to perform. And therefore 'it was accounted to him for righteousness'" (Romans 4:20-22, explanation added). In other words, Abraham didn't waver at God's promise to make his descendants as many as the stars of the sky. He didn't question how God was going to do it. Instead, he praised God and, through his praise, was strengthened in faith and became fully convinced God was able to perform what He had promised.

That's a good challenge for you and me. When we look into God's Word and see His promises, are we fully convinced they apply to us? Or do we believe they apply only to others?

When You Believed

A common problem among Christians is they're not fully convinced of what God's Word says because it doesn't line up with the way they think about or see themselves. Abraham could have easily done the same thing. He was close to one hundred years old and had no children of his own when God made him this promise. But Abraham decided not to look at his circumstances and instead believed God. It was at this point the Bible says God accounted it to him for righteousness.

Remember, righteousness is right-standing with God, including the ability to stand before Him without guilt or inferiority as if you had never sinned. God declared Abraham righteous simply because he believed Him.

This is all God asked of Abraham and it is all He ever asks of us.

In Isaiah 42:6, speaking of Jesus, God said, "I, the Lord, have called You to demonstrate my righteousness. I will take you by the hand and guard you, and I will give you to my people, Israel, as a symbol of my covenant with them. And you will be a light to guide the nations" (NLT). Similar to the covenant God made with Abraham, God established a new covenant through His Son Jesus with us.

God's part of the covenant is the provision of salvation and eternal life. Our part of the covenant is to believe on Him for the forgiveness of sins. To be born again, we have to believe God and His promise of salvation. Just as Abraham believed and it was accounted to him for righteousness, when we believe God and accept Jesus as our Savior, it is accounted to us for righteousness. This means at the moment of salvation, you and I are given right standing with God, the ability to stand before Him without any guilt or inferiority as if we had never sinned!

It doesn't matter if you've been born-again for 15 years, 53 years, or 5 months, your righteousness began the moment you believed and accepted Jesus as your savior. Let me prove this to you.

To receive salvation, you had to confess and believe. The Bible says, "If you confess with your mouth the Lord Jesus and believe in your heart that God has raised Him from the dead, you will be saved" (Romans 10:9). But upon our believing, God gives us so much more than just a ticket to heaven. Romans 10:10 continues speaking of salvation: "For with the heart one believes unto righteousness, and with the mouth confession is made unto salvation." Just like Abraham "believed in the Lord, and He accounted it to him for righteousness," when we confess Jesus as our Lord and believe that God raised Him from the dead, it is also accounted to us, "for with the heart one believes unto righteousness." If Jesus took care of the sin, then upon believing, we are given His righteousness! This takes place at the moment of salvation—the very moment we believe.

You've Been Justified

Let's look again at Paul's account of Abraham. He said, "And therefore 'it was accounted to him [Abraham] for righteousness.' Now it was not written for his sake alone that it was imputed to him, but also for us. It shall be imputed to us who believe in Him who raised up Jesus our Lord from the dead, who was delivered up because of our offenses, and was raised because of our justification" (Romans 4:22-25). The Apostle Paul is speaking of righteousness. In other words, the story of Abraham and how he received right-standing with God was not written so we could put him on a pedestal and marvel at his faith. It was written so we would understand the same righteousness shall be imputed (meaning imparted or given) to us who believe.

Notice another big-sounding word in the passage from Romans 4 that is very important: *justification*. Justification is God's declaration that the believing sinner is righteous and acceptable before Him.[1]

But hold on. Can you be a "believing sinner?" These two words together almost sound like an oxymoron, yet the answer is yes, you can be a "believing sinner," but only for one moment in time. What God calls a "believing sinner" is a sinner (someone who has not yet believed in Jesus) who *now* believes. This is a very accurate picture of what takes place at salvation: We were sinners who had no righteousness, but upon receiving Jesus as our Savior, we became believers with righteousness. At the very moment we asked Jesus in our heart, there was a transformation that took place where, on our way to becoming a believer, we were a sinner first, thus making us for one moment in time a "believing sinner."

It was at that moment that justification took place, making the new believer righteous and acceptable before God. That's when the title changed.

As soon as you accept Jesus as your Savior, you are no longer a believing sinner. You are now the righteousness of God in Christ, regardless of how you feel about it. I know you may be thinking, "Can I say that? Can I really say I'm the righteousness of God in Christ?" Yes, God's Word said it first.

We struggle with this thought because we're aware of our faults and failures. It seems prideful and wrong to apply something to ourselves that befits Jesus more than us. But let me ask you this: Is it okay to say Jesus took our sin? We don't see Him as a sinner, but the fact remains He became something He was not. According to 2 Corinthians 5:21, just as God made Jesus become sin, He has made you righteous—something you were not, but now are in Him.

CHAPTER NINE

Misunderstood Revelation

What use is revelation or religion if it doesn't change anything?

-Bakir Bashir

D o you recall the story of Daniel and his experience in the lion's den, as recounted in Daniel 6? It all started because Daniel was a righteous man who prayed night and day to his God. As an advisor to King Darius, he found favor with the king, making the other advisors jealous. These other men proposed an idea to King Darius to build a monument in his image and decree that all people should bow down and worship it. They also proposed that all who would not bow down be thrown into the lion's den.

Can't He Change His Mind?

The idea pleased the king, so he made the declaration. When Daniel was accused of not bowing down to the idol because of his love for and commitment to God, the king's decree meant that he must be thrown to the lions. But King Darius loved Daniel very much. You would think that he, being the king, could change his mind and save Daniel from this awful punishment, but he could not. Once a decree had been made by the king, it could not be changed.

God is our king and, as it was with the decree of King Darius, once the king declares a believing sinner to be righteous and acceptable before Him, it cannot be changed. This is why, although we wrestle with understanding God's acceptance of us in spite of our sins and shortcomings, our struggle doesn't change His view.

In the last chapter, we said justification is God's declaration that the believing sinner is righteous and acceptable before Him. Our God is a righteous Judge. When He sees a sinner receiving Jesus as their Savior, our righteous Judge stands up from His throne, smiles and declares, "That child is mine—righteous and acceptable before Me!" And when God declares something, it is settled in heaven.

Make sure you have a clear picture of what took place at salvation. God made Jesus, who knew no sin, to become sin so we could become righteous and acceptable before Him when we believe He raised His Son from the dead. I am bothered by Christians who say, "Well, I'm just a sinner saved by grace." I used to have a similar mentality, but this is not what the Bible teaches. The Bible says, "For by grace you have been saved through faith, and that not of yourselves; it is the gift of God, not of works, lest anyone should boast" (Ephesians 2:8-9).

God declares that the believing sinner is righteous and acceptable before Him. In that one moment in time, when you were a "believing sinner," God declared you to be righteous and acceptable before Him. Because of God's declaration, you can now stand before Him without any guilt or inferiority as if you had never been a sinner in the first place.

On the day I finally understood this, I rejoiced! The truth was, when I was born-again, I was declared righteous. The same is true for you! If you were born again yesterday, God declared you righteous. If you were born again 53 years ago, God declared you righteous 53 years ago! The Bible clearly says the believer is righteous and acceptable before God without any guilt, as if he or she never sinned. This righteousness was given to us by God's declaration the moment we received Jesus as our Savior, but many of us have journeyed on this Christian walk not feeling one bit righteous.

Beginner Basics

I remember the first time I was tempted to pick up the unforgiveness and condemnation I had laid down in front of my mirror. It's not so much that I remember exactly what it was I had done to make me feel guilty, but more that I remember the struggle of being tempted to beat myself up again.

Philippians 1:6 says we can be "confident of this very thing, that He who has begun a good work in you will complete it until the day of Jesus Christ." In my moment of weakness and self-condemnation, the Holy Spirit reminded me, "There is therefore now no condemnation to those who are in Christ Jesus" (Romans 8:1).

I wasn't entirely sure what this phrase meant, but as I told you earlier, I began to quote it often nonetheless. With each confession, my temptation to pick up what I had laid down was lessened.

I later realized a bigger problem was that I didn't recognize what the Holy Spirit said to me as scripture from the Bible! I was certainly a babe in Christ. This is a problem with many Christians, even those who have been born again for years. They might recognize a scripture from the Bible, but they can't tell you where it's from, or quote it on their own, much less explain it. Paul said in Hebrews 5:12, "You have been believers so long now that you ought to be teaching others. Instead, you need someone to teach you again the basic things about God's word" (NLT).

E.W. Kenyon once said, "All believers are in Christ, but [unfortunately] His Word is not in all believers."[1] This is sad but true. The beginner basics found in God's Word such as discovering God loves us and has forgiven all our sins, discovering and understanding how we've been made new creatures in Christ, and realizing that when we make a mistake there's no condemnation for those who are in Christ Jesus, are the foundations of victorious living for every Christian. If we don't learn these principles and begin to renew our minds accordingly, we not only remain in the beginner stage permanently, but we are also perfect prey for the enemy.

> *The spiritual is parent of the practical.*
> *-Thomas Carlyle*

It's a true statement that if we continue doing what we have always done, we will continue having what we've always had. For instance, I was guilty of condemning myself. Although every mistake, every failure, and every ungodly thing I had committed in my past was forgiven by God the moment I was born again, I continued to condemn myself for not knowing better. Ephesians 1:7 says, "In Him we have redemption through His blood, the forgiveness of sins, according to the riches of His grace." This grace was hard to accept. I struggled to accept the good news that every mistake and failure made after accepting Jesus as my Savior was also forgiven each time I went to God to confess my sins.

You Are Forgiven

First John 1:9 is a scripture you should never forget! It says, "If we confess our sins, He is faithful and just to forgive us our sins and to cleanse us from all unrighteousness." This is a promise to born-again believers. Every time our heart is pierced with recognition of sin and our lips whisper, "I'm sorry God," He is faithful to forgive our sins and wash them from His sight.

God's people are destroyed for a lack of knowledge (Hosea 4:6). If we don't know that God's Word says we are forgiven when we confess, then it is only natural to pick up the ugly feelings of guilt and condemnation, again.

Revelation of Right and Wrong

Knowledge can make us or break us. Because I didn't begin learning God's Word until I was already an adult (and had by that time committed more sins than I cared to count), my knowledge of sin tipped the scales in the wrong direction. I believed it was my past sins that kept me from having a closer relationship with

God, so I was quite surprised to discover the great Apostle Paul was tempted to feel the same way. He said, "I felt fine when I did not understand what the law demanded. But when I learned the truth, I realized I had broken the law and was a sinner, doomed to die. So the good law, which was supposed to show me the way of life, instead gave me the death penalty" (Romans 7:9-10, TLB). Like me, Paul struggled with the knowledge of sin mixed with his understanding of God's commandments.

I think we can all relate. Once we are born again, our eyes are opened to a huge revelation of right and wrong, which we didn't fully understand previously (if at all). Before we began hearing God's Word and its list of do's and don'ts, we were fine. But, as Paul said, when we found out what we were supposed to be doing and learned God's definition of sin, instead of bringing life or freedom, we found death.

Death is defined as separation from God, so in this case, Paul is referring to anything that separates us—including guilt and condemnation.

> So the good law, which was supposed to show me the way of life, instead gave me the death penalty. Sin took advantage of the law and fooled me; it took the good law and used it to make me guilty of death. But still, the law itself is holy and right and good. But how can that be? Did the law, which is good, cause my doom? Of course not! Sin used what was good to bring about my condemnation. So we can see how terrible sin really is. It uses God's good commandment for its own evil purposes.
>
> Romans 7:10-13, TLB

Shame and guilt are never God's intention for the believer. Revelations contained in God's Word are intended to bring recognition of sin to our minds so we can turn from it. But our enemy, the devil, twists new revelations of right and wrong with the memory of our past, thus making our sin appear exceedingly sinful in our own mind. This then piles guilt and condemnation on our shoulders unnecessarily.

Condemnation vs. Conviction

One thing we all need to understand, though, is that the automatic result of sin is condemnation. In Romans 5:18, Paul said, "Yes, Adam's one sin brought condemnation for everyone" (NLT). In other words, through Adam's disobedience to God, judgment and condemnation came to all men. This judgment was an inherited sin nature that separated us from God. But God's plan was for reconciliation, not condemnation.

Satan brought sin into this world, and condemnation is part of his package. God's desire is to have all mankind reconciled back to Him and to have close fellowship with His children. But without a clear revelation of the reconciliation God brought to us at salvation, the feeling of condemnation that comes from sin is apt to stay.

After we are born again, the Holy Spirit begins to deal with us regarding sin in the form of conviction. Conviction is a gentle pull on the inside, tugging us to make changes and adjustments in our life. Condemnation, on the other hand, is an ugly, harsh voice (not from God) that causes us to feel like a failure when we recognize sin in our lives. It's a continual battle for believers, who have no knowledge of who they are in Christ, to get out of this cycle of condemnation.

The problem is we try to fit into the mold of a "good Christian," yet inevitably fail because of sin. Condemnation then creeps in, attempting to keep us defeated. We may get victory over it for a while, but it isn't long before we are tempted to pick it back up, believing that little devil on our shoulder who keeps reminding us of our failures.

Naturally Speaking

The Bible says, "The natural man does not receive the things of the Spirit of God, for they are foolishness to him; nor can he know them, because they are spiritually discerned (1 Corinthians 2:14). Upon accepting Jesus as our Savior, we are given a new nature. This new nature is found within us. Our hair and skin color or features don't change because these are all part of our outward man. When Paul said, "If anyone is in Christ, he is a new creation; old things have passed away; behold, all things have become new" (2 Corinthians 5:17), he was referring to the awakening of our spirit, which now bears witness with God's Spirit.

The natural man is part of the old that passed away. In other words, whereas before salvation our natural man ruled everything, now after salvation, the natural man has a new master—our spirit, which bears witness with God's Spirit. The problem however, is that part of the natural man is our mind, will, and emotions, which are not automatically renewed to the things of God; they must be transformed through continual feeding and monitoring. This is the reason our minds are attacked so often by the enemy.

He plants suggestive thoughts that seem to make sense to our natural mind because the "natural man does not receive the things of the Spirit of God." The things of God are foolishness to the natural man, and the devil loves to take advantage of this fact.

For the most part, a large majority of the body of Christ is comprised of a sense knowledge group of people who lean more on their understanding and how they feel than on their ability to discern the things of the Spirit. This is why it is so easy for the devil to put condemnation on believers. It makes sense that we should feel guilty for our sins. We have failed to train our spirits to discern and correctly evaluate our surroundings and circumstances based on God's Word.

Hebrews says, "For everyone who partakes only of milk is unskilled in the word of righteousness, for he is a babe. But solid food belongs to those who are of full age, that is, those who by reason of use have their senses exercised to discern both good and evil" (Hebrews 5:13-14). This is interesting. Believers receive a new nature upon salvation, but that nature is a baby, regardless of how old the natural man or woman is.

To be fully grown and skilled in righteousness, the believer has to, by reason of use, exercise their senses to discern what is of God and what is not. (A good example is learning to discern between condemnation and conviction.) In the natural, children learn by reason of use as they experiment and grow, no matter how many times they fail along the way. This principle is the same for spiritual things. Having a revelation of right and wrong and then discerning correctly between condemnation and conviction dictates the rate of our growth in Christ.

Paul told Timothy, "Be diligent to present yourself approved to God, a worker who does not need to be ashamed, rightly dividing the word of truth" (2 Timothy 2:15). The *King James Version* says, "Study to show thyself approved." This aspect of our walk with God is vital to our growth because although we can be sincere, we can also be sincerely wrong. However, with practice, we can correctly analyze the word of truth and use it to override how we feel or what we think about ourselves.

When we lean not on our own understanding, but in all our ways acknowledge God (Proverbs 3:5-6) and His way of doing things (Matthew 6:33), we are actually learning to discern correctly. When this happens, our new man can receive the things of the Spirit of God, for they are not foolishness to him; he can know them, because they are spiritually discerned.

As I began to study God's Word and pursue His truth, I finally found the scripture the Holy Spirit prompted me to say each time I was tempted to hold on to my guilt: "There is therefore now no condemnation for those who are in Christ Jesus." Ironically, this verse was written by the Apostle Paul in Romans 8:1, right after he confessed having his own struggle with guilt.

CHAPTER TEN

Resisting Condemnation

Compassion will cure more sins than condemnation.
-Henry Ward Beecher

A friend of mine was recently feeling a bit condemned because she had struggled with thoughts of quitting something that was in her best interest. She hadn't quit, but was still mad at herself for even entertaining the thoughts. I reminded her that she was a three-part being.

In 1 Thessalonians 4:17, the Bible says we are spirit, soul, and body. The body is the house where our spirit and soul resides. The spirit is the part of us that is born again and in contact with God, and the soul is the realm of our mind, will, and emotions. My friend was feeling guilty over the thought of quitting, when in reality, those thoughts were simply the conversation between her soul and spirit. I enthusiastically reminded her that her spirit had won because she hadn't quit.

The Apostle Paul said, "I say then: Walk in the Spirit, and you shall not fulfill the lust of the flesh. For the flesh lusts against the Spirit, and the Spirit against the flesh; and these are contrary to one another, so that you do not do the things that you wish" (Galatians 5:16-17). In other words, when the flesh (or we could say, our soul) is in spiritual warfare with our spirit (the part of us that belongs to God), one or the other is going to win—but not both.

Dominant Identity

Inside of every believer, there are two identities, and they are completely opposite of one another. It would help us to picture these two constantly fighting and warring with each another until one finally submits. Over time, the identity that is strongest will become dominant while the weaker one becomes compliant and even docile. The word "docile" simply refers to something that is readily trained or taught. If the spirit of a man becomes the dominant identity, this is good. This means the flesh nature of the man has become compliant and even readily trained to submit.

However, if these are reversed and the flesh or soul, is the dominant identity, this can be bad. Instead of being spirit-led, this person is controlled by their mind, will, and emotions. This is what Paul meant when he said, "For what I am doing, I do not understand. For what I will to do, that I do not practice; but what I hate, that I do" (Romans 7:15). The emotions and decisions made by the flesh turn on you and what felt good in the moment, is now the cause of guilt and condemnation. Why? Because the flesh lusts against the spirit, and the two are contrary to one another.

People often wonder, "Well, how will I know if I'm in the flesh or in the spirit?" The Bible gives us a full-proof test. Galatians 5:22-23 says, "Now the fruit of the Spirit is love, joy, peace, longsuffering, kindness, goodness, faithfulness, gentleness, and self-control." If a person can recognize these in operation in his life, this is then proof of being led by the spirit. Conversely, if there is a lack of these, this is proof of being led by the flesh.

Of all the fruit of the Spirit, self-control is the one we must pay attention to the most because all the others will be evident if we keep a tab on this one. Self-control simply means you are allowing the real you on the inside to call all the shots. We could call it "spirit-controlled." In other words, when our mind, will, and emotions are fighting us, the battle will be won when we allow our spirit to have the last word.

The flesh and the spirit are hungry. Whichever one we choose to feed the most will be the stronger of the two. People are often discouraged because when they want to do good, they can't seem to. In those cases, it would be good to ask, "What have you been feeding your spirit lately?" My friend was frustrated with the fight within her, but what she didn't realize was she must have been feeding her spirit because her flesh didn't win. Yet, in her limited knowledge, she still entertained condemnation unnecessarily.

> *Guilt is perhaps the most painful companion to death.*
> *-Coco Chanel*

The Bible says when sin entered the world through Adam and Eve, judgment came to all men from that point forward. "Therefore, as through one man's offense judgment came to all men, resulting in condemnation, even so through one Man's righteous act the free gift came to all men, resulting in justification of life" (Romans 5:18). In other words, we're all born with a sin nature, which automatically produces condemnation. But after salvation, any struggle the believer has with condemnation is never from God. (I repeat, never.)

God's correction always comes through conviction—not condemnation. "There is therefore now no condemnation for those who are in Christ Jesus" (Romans 8:1). Condemnation is applied to the non-believer, while conviction is applied to the believer. John 3:18 says, "He who believes in Him is not condemned; but he who does not believe is condemned already, because he has not believed in the name of the only begotten Son of God."

Without a clear revelation of what the believer received when he or she was born again (forgiveness and right-standing with God), condemnation is apt to stay. In other words, the devil will convince you it is natural to feel condemned for sin, because in his words "you are guilty and unworthy." Let me ask you this question: Are you born again? If the answer is yes, then you are in Christ Jesus and the Bible says, "There is no condemnation **for those who are in Christ Jesus,** who do not walk according to the flesh" (Romans 8:1-2, emphasis added).

Our flesh is comprised of those feelings and desires that are governed by our mind, will, and emotions. Paul is stating there is no condemnation for those who do not walk or live life according to their feelings. So would the opposite be true? Yes, most definitely. There is a door for condemnation for those who live life always following their feelings.

I've told you before, I was guilty of condemning myself because I was governed every day by my own feelings of unworthiness and insecurity. I lived under a huge cloud of condemnation all the time. I never felt I could do anything right. But God wasn't responsible for my wrong thinking. I made a choice to follow my feelings, which opened the door for condemnation from the devil.

John 4:24 says, "God is Spirit and those who worship Him must worship in spirit and truth." God's Word is truth. There is no condemnation for those who walk according to the Spirit and according to what God has said in His Word.

Baffled

Looking at Paul's life, we discover he had a strong revelation of who he was in Christ. In fact, inspired by the Holy Spirit, Paul wrote more of the New Testament than any other person. Yet this same man confessed he struggled in the flesh. He had been given a new nature through salvation, but his fleshly desires were constantly at war with his new nature. This is a struggle we can identify with. From the moment we wake up each day until we go to bed each night, our new nature battles with the desires of our flesh, or our feelings.

If our minds aren't renewed in God's Word regarding our right-standing with Him, we will naturally allow our feelings to override God's Word. Paul said he was baffled because he couldn't seem to practice or accomplish what he wished, but instead did the things he actually loathed (and later felt guilty for). He also admitted he was tempted to believe his feelings. He said, "O wretched man that I am! Who will deliver me from this body of death?" (Romans 7:24).

Does that sound familiar? Have your feelings ever said something similar?

"I'm pitiful."

"I don't know why I try."

"I can't do anything right."

Like Paul, often that's how we want to feel, but it's not the truth. And Paul knew this too. He admitted his feelings, but then immediately made a choice not to follow how he felt because he knew it was contrary to God's Word. He said "O wretched man that I am! Who will deliver me from this body of death? I thank God—through Jesus Christ our Lord! So then, with the **mind** I myself serve the law of God, but with the **flesh** the law of sin" (Romans 7:24-25, emphasis added). Paul fully realized his flesh, or feelings, would always choose the law of sin. But with his mind, he could make a choice to serve the law of God, consciously deciding to follow what God said about him instead of what his feelings were telling him.

Paul said, "I was alive once without the law, but when the commandment came, sin revived and I died. And the commandment, which was to bring life, I found to bring death" (Romans 7:9-10). He wasn't talking about literal death here. He was describing how he felt regarding the conflict between his flesh and his new nature in Christ. In other words, the Word that was supposed to bring him life or freedom he found brought death or condemnation. His understanding of sin left him feeling guilty.

But God, through the Holy Spirit, enlightened his understanding regarding the difference between following after the flesh and following after the Spirit. "For those who live according to the flesh set their minds on the things of the flesh, but those who live according to the Spirit, the things of the Spirit. For to be carnally minded is death, but to be spiritually minded is life and peace" (Romans 8:5-6). In other words, those who constantly think and meditate on their feelings (or flesh) will live according to or be dominated by those feelings. The *Amplified Bible* describes the death that arises from being carnally minded as that which "comprises all the miseries arising from sin." For example, if our feelings are filled with guilt, condemnation, low self-esteem, or unworthiness, then we will live in relation to those miserable feelings.

On the other hand, if we'll begin to meditate and constantly think on what God's Word says about us and who we are in Christ, our feelings will work in the positive instead of the negative. We have the promise of life and peace if we will just set our minds on the things of the Spirit. But if we decide to believe and trust only in our feelings, then we will live our entire life according to those feelings, never finding true peace. To be carnally minded simply means our sinful nature is in control. According to God's Word, the only thing that can come from a carnal mindset is death or condemnation.

Faith and Feelings

In the eyes of God, when I confessed Jesus as my Lord and Savior, I was a new creation endowed with righteousness. However, my feelings about myself dictated otherwise, and so, I let my feelings dominate me.

We need to understand that righteousness is never based on our feelings.

God's Word never changes. However, our feelings change constantly, depending on our circumstances. If our faith is in our feelings, which do change, then our faith will imitate our feelings by constantly changing. But if our faith is in God's Word, which never changes, then our faith won't waver, regardless of our circumstances or our feelings.

The good news is that those who make a decision to believe and trust in the Word of God—regardless of what their feelings say—will live according to the Spirit in abundant life and peace, for "There is therefore now no condemnation for those who are in Christ Jesus, who do not walk according to the flesh, but according to the Spirit" (Romans 8:1-2).

As we attempt to reflect Christ as accurately as possible, it is important that our spirits become more in tune with God's Word. Righteousness is first a position we've been given in Christ, and then the actions that follow. This includes resisting condemnation and moving forward after repentance.

CHAPTER ELEVEN

Engrafted

A man finds his identity by identifying.
-Robert Terwilliger

L ike every little girl, when I was growing up, I had a "BFF"—a best friend forever. Her name was Tori. She and I were about the same height and weight, and we both had blonde hair. It didn't matter if we were with her mom or my mom, people would always ask if we were twins. I realize now it had little to do with our physical similarities. We spent so much time together as young girls that we actually began to act like one another. Our mannerisms were the same, and we could finish each other's sentences because we also thought the same.

Becoming Like Him

The Bible says, "For He made Him who knew no sin to be sin for us, that we might become the righteousness of God in Him" (2 Corinthians 5:21). In other words, there was a great exchange.

Jesus took our sin (becoming sin for us), and we took His righteousness (becoming like Him).

Another aspect of our new life in Christ involves being engrafted in Him. In horticulture, the word engrafted refers to a cut made in the stem of a plant wherein another plant with an identical cut is placed in the slot so the two combine and grow as one. Engrafting is generally only successful between two closely related species.

The book of James tells us to, "Receive with meekness the **engrafted** word, which is able to save your souls" (1:21, KJV, emphasis added). As I've already mentioned, the soul of a person is their mind, will, and emotions. Before receiving Christ, our soul leans toward sinful tendencies. After salvation however, our soul is constantly in the process of being renewed to the image and nature of Christ. Therefore, God's Word is vital when it comes to rescuing our soul (our mind, will, and emotions) from danger, possible harm, injury, or loss. This alone, is enough reason to cling to God's Word. It saves us from us.

So consider the word engrafted, and think again about its meaning. Engrafting describes a cut made in one species so another closely related species can be placed in the cut, blended and grown with the dominant source, thus resulting in one new creation. James said God's Word is engrafted into those who will receive it, but this is not always an easy or painless task. "For the word of God is living and powerful, and sharper than any two-edged sword, piercing even to the division of soul and spirit, and of joints and morrow, and is a discerner of the thoughts and intents of the heart" (Hebrews 4:12). The word engrafted includes the idea of being wounded. God's Word has been known to step on toes and address areas we'd rather leave undisturbed. But remember, the goal is to rescue us from our own mind, will, and emotions, which are a constant playground for Satan.

The psalmist said, "O GOD... deal with me for Your name's sake... I am poor and needy, and my heart is wounded within me" (Psalm 109:21-22). In his prayer, he specifically asked God to check him. Then he said his heart (the part of us with which God deals) was wounded within him.

When we acknowledge our need and make ourselves vulnerable to God by being honest and open with Him, His Word then inserts itself in the wound of our brokenness, binding itself to our heart to add life and bring growth. This is really amazing because successful engrafting can only take place between two closely related species. Remember, Christians are new creations in Christ Jesus. As such, they have taken on His nature, becoming like Him.

Forgiveness is the fragrance that the violet sheds on the heel that has crushed it.
-Mark Twain

But that's not all! Using horticulture as our example again, when a plant is engrafted into another, it is very common for one plant to sprout and produce the blooms of the other species on its own stems. As a Christian, you are called to produce "fruits of righteousness" (Philippians 1:11). In other words, as you allow His Word to address and remove your shame, guilt, and pain, the wounds these areas leave behind soon become a branch overflowing with the blooms of God's nature.

This is what I tried to explain to Benjamin as a young boy who was already tempted to dislike who he was. He was made in the image of God, and so was my friend who struggled with homosexuality. Despite how either of them felt, their faith in Christ and understanding of God's Word, *mixed with time,* would reveal God's nature in them eventually.

There's one more important fact we need to understand about the engrafting process: Jesus was wounded first. The prophet Isaiah said, "Surely He has borne our griefs and carried our sorrows; yet we esteemed Him stricken, smitten by God, and afflicted. But He was wounded for our transgressions, He was bruised for our iniquities; the chastisement for our peace was upon Him, and by His stripes we are healed" (Isaiah 53:4-5).

Remember, this was God's plan. When Jesus took our sins, a spiritual cut was made, which allowed us to be placed in Him. If He had not been wounded, there would have been no cut and no place for us to be grafted in. Yet now, because He fulfilled the righteous requirement, we have the privilege of allowing His nature to overtake our nature so others will see Him in us.

Renewing Our Minds

The reason these truths are sometimes hard to accept is because we have given more weight to the world's way of doing things than God's way. Paul said in Romans 12:2, "Do not be conformed to this world, but be transformed by the renewing of your mind that you may prove what is that good and acceptable and perfect will of God." For example, God's forgiveness of our sins when we give our lives to Jesus transforms how He sees us. He no longer sees the sins we've committed. But we often continue seeing ourselves the same way we did before we were born again—through the eyes of guilt, condemnation, and comparison—because our minds have not yet been renewed to God's Word.

After I received salvation, I continued to struggle with insecurities and fears in my attempts to fit into a new mold, desperately wanting to be accepted by God and others. But in God's eyes, I was already a new creature in Christ. I just couldn't see it because my mind had not yet been renewed to these truths. I carried all the same mentalities and struggles I had had in the world into my walk with Christ, trying to fit them into a new package, that of a Christian.

This is true of most new believers who don't know how they measure up in God's eyes. Sometimes they attempt to figure it out by observing other believers, but sadly, that's not a full-proof plan because others may be just as lost when it comes to their identity in Christ. The best place to discover who you are in Christ is by His example and as described in His Word.

When we receive salvation (are engrafted into Christ), faith is birthed in our hearts based on the message of God's grace, love, and forgiveness. Yet because we know what we've done and what God is actually offering to forgive, we struggle with these truths. But God's Word encourages us to believe, regardless of how we feel or what we think true justice should look like.

Forgiven

Are you familiar with the Bible story of the woman caught in adultery? You and I may or may not have ever been in shoes like hers, but nonetheless, in our own mind, our sin is just as hard to bear. Let's look at this story not just as a picture of initial salvation, but also as a true depiction of God's continuing love, understanding, and instruction.

Early in the morning (at dawn), He came back into the temple [court], and the people came to Him in crowds. He sat down and was teaching them when the scribes and Pharisees brought a woman who had been caught in adultery. They made her stand in the middle of the court and put the case before Him. "Teacher," they said, "This woman has been caught in the very act of adultery. Now Moses in the Law commanded us that such [women—offenders] shall be stoned to death. But what do You say [to do with her—what is Your sentence]?"

This they said to try (test) Him, hoping they might find a charge on which to accuse Him.

But Jesus stooped down and wrote on the ground with His finger. However, when they persisted with their question, He raised Himself up and said, "Let him who is without sin among you be the first to throw a stone at her." Then He bent down and went on writing on the ground with His finger. They listened to Him, and then they began going out, conscience-stricken, one by one, from the oldest down to the last one of them, till Jesus was left alone, with the woman standing there before Him in the center of the court.

When Jesus raised Himself up, He said to her, "Woman, where are your accusers? Has no man condemned you?" She answered, "No one, Lord!" And Jesus said, "I do not condemn you either. Go on your way and from now on sin no more" (John 8:2-11, AMP).

Did you hear Him correctly?

Do you realize this is still what the Lord is saying today? "Go and sin no more."

When the devil, our own conscience, or anyone else brings an accusation against us, do you realize God's first reaction to us is the same as Jesus had with this woman? "Go and sin no more." She was guilty, but Jesus showed compassion. He didn't condone her sin by understanding it; He simply revealed the nature and heart of God by not condemning her.

Many theologians believe when Jesus was writing in the dirt with his finger, that He was identifying the sins of those in the crowd. As their conscience was pricked, they left one by one. The truth is, when we find ourselves guilty of sin, we should be bruised with sorrow over it. In other words, just because God offers grace doesn't mean we should take it lightly. But at the same time, we need to understand the heart of God is compassionate even as it is holy and His desire is to teach us, because unfortunately we will fail again. But He knows we have been engrafted with His nature, and patience is required. The fruit of righteousness will show up eventually.

What Jesus said to the woman is what He is still saying to us today, "Go and sin no more." This is our instruction. It means, "Learn your lesson. Receive forgiveness. Don't do it again."

Many times I have had to go to God in prayer and express my sincere remorse for failing again at something I felt I knew better than to do. Failing again at the same thing didn't necessarily mean I was taking forgiveness for granted. On the contrary, it meant I was growing. The danger would be if I committed the same sin again and again but I wasn't grieved by it. Just as a child learning to walk stumbles and picks herself back up, only to stumble again as her legs grow stronger, we sometimes fail because our spiritual legs are weak. God understands this, and it is why He says again and again, "Go and sin no more."

Our response should be, "Yes, Lord." And then our actions should match our words. When sin is revealed in our lives, we should repent. The word "repent" is defined in the Greek as to think differently. Repentance isn't just an action; it's also a mental decision. It insinuates we must first recognize the wrong in our life before we can change it. The Apostle Paul said, "Don't copy the behavior and customs of this world, but let God transform you into a new person **by changing the way you think.** Then you will learn to know God's will for you, which is good and pleasing and perfect" (Romans 12:2, emphasis added).

We can't change our past. But despite the remorse, guilt, and temptations of our flesh, we can be changed. "We have the mind of Christ" (1 Corinthians 2:16), and therefore, we are infused with His nature and His righteousness.

CHAPTER TWELVE

Performance Not Required

The wheel's spinning, but the hamster's dead.
                                        -Author Unknown

It was a little scary for me when Benjamin turned 16 years old and got his driver's license, but it was also fun to watch him grow up and become a man. One day his truck was giving him some trouble and seemed to be low on oil, so he began tinkering around on it in our front driveway. His dad was out of town, so there were several phone calls back and forth in an attempt to fix the problem, all while I was inside doing laundry.

More than Sweat

Some time later, Benjamin came in to say that he thought his truck was fixed, and he added, "Oh, by the way, Mom, can you wash this shirt? I need it for athletics tomorrow." He proceeded to toss me a grey t-shirt, which I quickly added to a load I was just putting in the washer. Afterward, when the same load came

119

out of the dryer, I pulled out the grey t-shirt to fold, only then to notice it had big stains all over it. About that time, Benjamin walked by, and I asked if the school had given the shirt to him like that. His response? "No, I used it to check my oil."

What? Not only was this the wrong thing to use to check oil, but I had just thrown it into my washer thinking the only thing it carried was teenage sweat!

This incident reminds me of Isaiah 64:5, which says, "But we are all like an unclean thing, and all our righteousnesses are like filthy rags." There are two things to take away from this scripture. First, there is nothing we can do to earn our right standing with God. And second, once God has clothed us with His righteousness, we have a responsibility to keep it clean.

Let's look at earning our righteousness first. On our very best day, any good we've done is still a filthy rag in comparison to the price Jesus paid to cover our sins. The only way to receive righteousness is by faith and repentance. Romans 10:10 says, "For with the heart one believes unto righteousness." Paul said, "Now to him who works, the wages are not counted as grace but as debt. But to him who does not work but believes on Him who justifies the ungodly, his faith is accounted for righteousness, just as David also describes the blessedness of the man to whom God imputes righteousness apart from works" (Romans 4:4-6). All believers receive right-standing with God the day they are born again, the day they believe. So righteousness isn't something that is going to happen, nor is it something we are working towards or might someday attain because of our performance. No, righteousness is automatic the day we first believe in our heart and confess Jesus as our Lord.

There's Not Enough Good Works

The Bible says Abraham is the father of our faith, and he received righteousness because he believed God. We need to understand he didn't earn it. His right standing with God came through the righteousness of faith. "For the promise that he would be the heir of the world was not to Abraham or to his seed through the law, but through the righteousness of faith" (Romans 4:13).

The law refers to our works or performance. Too many Christians have the mentality that good works will eventually make them righteous. They sincerely believe righteousness is something they are working toward. "Well, if I can just get my act together and quit messing up all the time, then maybe some-day I'll be in right standing with God." Although it is important to live right and do our best not to sin, those things in and of themselves will not make you any more righteous than you already are.

Let me explain. I felt like I couldn't reach God because I was trapped in a box of unforgiveness, and I had no knowledge of what Jesus had done for me or how God saw me through Him. I tried very hard to reach God through my works, by fitting into a certain mold. Out of desperation, I started praying and asking for God's help. I needed revelation. Just as I had worked hard in the world to fit in, I was working very hard at being a perfect Christian, but was getting nowhere.

At one point, God encouraged me to be the best I knew how to be, and it was good and right for me to focus on those things. I needed to get my eyes off my problems and on to Him. But God already knew I'd be spinning my wheels. My works were dead, getting me nowhere, but I kept working anyway.

The funny thing is, God doesn't allow us to walk through things so He can see what we're made of; He already knows. He allows us to walk through things so we can see what we're made of. I needed to see how my entire life had been built on works.

Righteousness is received by faith, not by the things we do or don't do. Concerning Abraham, Paul said, "What then shall we say that Abraham our father has found according to the flesh? For if Abraham was justified by works, he has something to boast about, but not before God. For what does the Scripture say? 'Abraham believed God, and it was accounted to him for righteousness.' Now to him who works, the wages are not counted as grace but as debt. But to him who does not work but believes on Him who justifies the ungodly, his faith is accounted for righteousness" (Romans 4:1-5). Basically, Paul was saying it was impossible for Abraham's works to bring him righteousness. Just like it is impossible for our works to bring us righteousness.

I like the way the *Living Bible* puts these verses: "Abraham was, humanly speaking, the founder of our Jewish nation. What were his experiences concerning this question of being saved by faith? Was it because of his good deeds that God accepted him? If so, he would have something to boast about. But from God's point of view Abraham had no basis at all for pride. For the Scriptures tell us Abraham believed God, and that is why God canceled his sins and declared him 'not guilty.' But didn't he earn his right to heaven by all the good things he did? No, for being saved is a gift; if a person could earn it by being good, then it wouldn't be free—but it is! It is given to those who do not work for it. For God declares sinners to be good in his sight if they have faith in Christ to save them from God's wrath."

Abraham believed God. That's it. And therefore, God gave him the gift of righteousness. It was nothing he could have earned through his works. The same is still true for us today.

The Righteousness of Faith

What's interesting is that God's chosen people, Israel, had been given the promise of a Savior and yet when the Savior came, they didn't believe in Him. Instead, they believed they had to earn their righteousness through the things they did. But the Gentiles, who were not God's chosen people, actually attained righteousness (right standing with God, including the ability to stand before Him without any guilt or inferiority as if they had never sinned) simply because they believed. "What shall we say then? That Gentiles, who did not pursue righteousness, have attained righteousness, even the righteousness of faith; but Israel, pursuing the law of righteousness, has not attained to the law of righteousness. Why? Because they did not seek it by **faith**, but as it were, by the works of the law" (Romans 9:30-32, emphasis added).

How many Christians today are doing exactly the same thing? I know in my ignorance, I tried to gain right-standing with God through the good things I did. In other words, I tried to earn it. But Paul said the promise was to Abraham and his seed through the righteousness of faith, not the law. There is nothing you or I could ever do to earn our righteousness. We must seek it by faith, meaning, we must believe. When we're ignorant of God's righteousness and seek to establish it on our own by the things we do instead of by faith, we've missed God's plan and forgotten our part of the covenant was always to believe.

Christ Didn't Die in Vain

Romans 10:3-4 says, "For they being ignorant of God's righteousness, and seeking to establish their own righteousness, have not submitted to the righteousness of God. For Christ is the end of the law for righteousness to everyone who believes." If we could earn our righteousness, then it wouldn't have been necessary for God to send His Son as the final sacrifice for our sins. But as it were, we were separated from God, with no hope, and in desperate need of a savior.

So it is by grace that we are saved. Ephesians 2:8-9 says, "For by grace you have been saved through faith, and that not of yourselves; it is the gift of God, not of works, lest anyone should boast." The key here is "through faith" we have been saved. If we could earn salvation through our performance, then what was the point of Jesus' death and resurrection? So why is righteousness any different?

Don't forget that it is at salvation, the moment we believe in Jesus, that we received our right standing with God. "I do not set aside the grace of God; for if righteousness comes through the law, then Christ died in vain" (Galatians 2:21). We have got to get over our works mentality. The number of times we go to church and the number of times we follow God's commandments is not going to increase our righteousness in God's eyes. His Word is established as a guideline for us to follow, and following His guidelines is always in our best interest. We absolutely need to follow His commandments. But righteousness is not something we are working towards. The bottom line is this:

For no one can ever be made right in God's sight by doing what the law commands. For the more we know God's laws, the clearer it becomes that we aren't obeying them; his laws serve only to make us see that we are sinners. But now God has shown us a different way to heaven—not by "being good enough" and trying to keep his laws, but by a new way (though not new, really, for the Scriptures told about it long ago). Now God says he will accept and acquit us—declare us "not guilty"—if we trust Jesus Christ to take away our sins. And we all can be saved in this same way, by coming to Christ, no matter who we are or what we have been like. Yes, all have sinned; all fall short of God's glorious ideal; yet now God declares us "not guilty" of offending him if we trust in Jesus Christ, who in his kindness freely takes away our sins. For God sent Christ Jesus to take the punishment for our sins and to end all God's anger against us. He used Christ's blood and our faith as the means of saving us from his wrath. In this way he was being entirely fair, even though he did not punish those who sinned in former times. For he was looking forward to the time when Christ would come and take away those sins. And now in these days also he can receive sinners in this same way because Jesus took away their sins.

Romans 3:20-26, TLB

God has given us His righteousness based on our faith. The Bible says, "I will greatly rejoice in the Lord, my soul shall be joyful in my God; for He has clothed me with the garments of salvation, He has covered me with the robe of righteousness" (Isaiah 61:10). God clothed us based on faith, not performance. But after the fact, it is true our righteousness should produce good works.

Keep it Clean

Referring to our attempts to earn salvation, Isaiah said, "But we are all like an unclean thing, and all our righteousnesses are like filthy rags" (Isaiah 64:5). But what if you received salvation and a robe of righteousness by faith and then still tried to live like you used to? I'm afraid that is only going to produce a filthy rag as well.

My son had been given a brand-new t-shirt for athletics. He was instructed to wear it at practice every day, as an identification. After the oil change incident, he still had to wear the same shirt, but now it had permanent grease marks all over it. His shirt still identified him from non-athletes, but what representation did his shirt now display?

This may be a silly example, but do you see the parallel? When God gives us right standing with Himself and puts a robe of righteousness on us, we now represent our King. Our robe of righteousness sets us apart from non-believers. But if we're not careful, our robes can become filthy through pride, works, sin, or even inferiority.

My own robe has been stained from poor judgment, flesh fits, and the like. Thankfully, God has a washing machine that cleanses from all unrighteousness! "If we [freely] admit that we have sinned and confess our sins, He is faithful and just (true to

His own nature and promises) and will forgive our sins [dismiss our lawlessness] and [continuously] cleanse us from all unrighteousness" (1 John 1:9, AMP).

This is a scripture we should quote, stand on, and depend on all the time! But listen to the instruction surrounding this promise: "This is the message which we have heard from Him and declare to you, that God is light and in Him is no darkness at all. If we say that we have fellowship with Him, and walk in darkness, we lie and do not practice the truth [we're not living what we claim]. But if we walk in the light as He is in the light, we have fellowship with one another, and the blood of Jesus Christ His Son cleanses us from all sin. If we say that we have no sin, we deceive ourselves, and the truth is not in us. If we confess our sins, He is faithful and just to forgive us our sins and to cleanse us from all unrighteousness. If we say that we have not sinned, we make Him a liar, and His word is not in us" (1 John 1:5-10, explanation added).

It is so important that we live what we claim. We must understand this is part of our righteousness as well. Otherwise, we make Him a liar and our robe of righteousness is nothing but a filthy rag. Remember, "When the kindness and the love of God our Savior toward man appeared, not by works of righteousness which we have done, but according to His mercy He saved us" (Titus 3:4-5). And because He saved us, we now represent Him every day. We are symbols of His Kingdom. If we fail (and we do sometimes), then let us acknowledge it to the only one who can cleanse us and put us back in right standing with Himself. God said, "No weapon formed against you shall prosper, and every tongue which rises against you in judgment you shall condemn. This is the heritage of the servants of the Lord, **and their righteousness is from Me,** says the Lord" (Isaiah 54:17, emphasis added).

CHAPTER THIRTEEN

Mirror, Mirror

There are two ways of spreading light: to be the candle or the mirror that reflects it.

-Edith Wharton

Mirror, Mirror, on the Wall
Who is really Lord of all?
Mirror, Mirror, on the Wall
Christ in me means hope for all.

This simple, yet powerfully truthful poem was written by my dear friend, Marie Myers. She and I have traveled together and ministered in the United States and overseas to women of all backgrounds. She is one of those special people who sharpens me. We both have similar stories of coming to Christ as adults, so we share a zeal for what it means to be made the righteousness of God in Christ.

On one trip, we sat in our hotel room like two schoolgirls having a slumber party, talking for hours about what Christ had done for us. As we shared, Marie said, "Some people's only hope of seeing Christ is through His reflection in us." In other words, God desires to reflect His glory through you and me, because the world isn't offering the right stuff.

Second Corinthians 3:18 says, "But we all, with unveiled face, beholding as in a mirror the glory of the Lord, are being transformed into the same image from glory to glory, just as by the Spirit of the Lord." Isn't it interesting that the Bible says we behold the glory of the Lord when we look in our mirrors? This was news to me. After giving my heart to Jesus, I can't say I saw anything that closely resembled Him or His glory when I looked in my mirror. But that was my perspective—not His.

To be unveiled means to take the mask off and truly reveal yourself. We know God can already see us (with or without a mask), so the instruction is directed more toward allowing others to see us. But we need to allow others not just to see us, meaning the fearful, insecure, or broken, but to see the new us—that which has been redeemed and repurposed for Christ. In other words, we need to allow others to see Him in us.

The *Amplified Bible* phrases this passage like this, "And all of us, as with unveiled face, [because we] continued to behold [in the Word of God] as in a mirror the glory of the Lord, are constantly being transfigured into His very own image in ever increasing splendor and from one degree of glory to another; [for this comes] from the Lord [Who is] the Spirit." The key word here is continued.

Without interruption or distraction, we need to face the mirror of God's Word and allow it to transform us.

Consider a mirror. It always accurately reflects or imitates what is put before it. The problem is, when God's Word is our mirror, we feel inferior at times. What we are reading in His Word and what our lives actually look like are often two totally different things.

But therein is also the solution! As we continue in God's Word, we are "constantly being transfigured into His very own image in ever increasing splendor and from one degree of glory to another." The mirror of God's Word isn't like the mirror in my bathroom. It has the unique ability to show me what God sees, not what I see.

To be transfigured or transformed describes something that happens from the inside out. *Christ is in us.* Therefore, with each decision we make to honor Him and His Word, He is revealed more and more through us. This is why the Bible says we are being changed into His image with ever increasing glory!

Notice this transformation takes place one decision at a time. In other words, every time I make a decision for righteousness, I become a mirror that shines brighter and brighter, reflecting Christ more and more. This doesn't just apply to what I believe about myself. Righteousness describes the new person God has made me—spirit, soul, and body. The Bible says, "You've become a new person. This new person is continually renewed in knowledge to be like its Creator. Where this happens, there is no Greek or Jew, circumcised or uncircumcised, barbarian, uncivilized person, slave or free person. Instead, Christ is everything and in everything" (Colossians 3:10-11, GW). In other words, it doesn't matter where you came from or what you've done, once you've accepted Christ, you are new on the inside. And eventually, that new should show up on the outside. For example, my decision to choose love, have patience, forgive others and myself, submit to authority, honor people, and be willing and ready to give to those in need despite my own needs, will reflect Christ in me.

Here's what the writer of Colossians went on to say:

> As holy people whom God has chosen and loved, be sympathetic, kind, humble, gentle, and patient. Put up with each other, and forgive each other if anyone has a complaint. Forgive as the Lord forgave you. Above all, be loving. This ties everything together perfectly. Also, let Christ's perfect peace control you. God has called you into this peace by bringing you into one body. Be thankful. Let Christ's word with all its wisdom and richness live in you. Use psalms, hymns, and spiritual songs to teach and instruct yourselves about God's kindness. Sing to God in your hearts. Everything you say or do should be done in the name of the Lord Jesus, giving thanks to God the Father through Him.
>
> Colossians 3:12-17, GW

Let me remind you that before you can ever truly reflect Christ toward others, you must first see Christ in you.

- Be kind, humble, gentle, and patient with yourself.
- Forgive yourself as the Lord has forgiven you.
- Love yourself, and let His peace control you.
- Be thankful, and let God reveal His kindness to you.

As Christians, we know these should be our actions toward others, but what does it say about God's Word when we withhold these same actions toward ourselves?

Mirror, Mirror, on the Wall
Who is really Lord of all?
Mirror, Mirror, on the Wall
Christ in me means hope for all!

Vessels of Honor

In my house, I have a beautiful vase in my entryway. It is set there to warmly greet my guests. We could say it is a vessel of honor. But in my kitchen, I have a trashcan, another vessel, but not as honorable. Both are in my house by my choice, and both serve a purpose. But in the real world, my trashcan can never decide it wants to be a vase. Its fate is sealed, and it will forever be a trashcan.

Did you know this is not so in the house of God?

The Apostle Paul said, "In a great house there are not only vessels of gold and silver, but also of wood and clay, some for honor and some for dishonor. Therefore if anyone cleanses himself from the latter, he will be a vessel for honor, sanctified and useful for the Master, prepared for every good work" (2 Timothy 2:20-21). The great house he spoke of is a depiction of God's house. In it, God has many types of vessels (describing those who have been welcomed in through faith in Christ). Notice that Paul said some vessels are for honor and

The face is the mirror of the mind, and eyes without speaking confess the secrets of the heart.
-St. Jerome

some for dishonor. A better translation is "...some for honorable and noble [use] and some for menial and ignoble [use]" (AMP). The word ignoble describes something of low character or low grade or quality, something inferior. This is often how we feel about ourselves when we come to Christ, and according to this scripture, if we don't make the necessary changes, this is how we'll remain.

But unlike my trashcan that is forever doomed to remain as such, you and I have a choice. As verse 21 tells us, "If anyone cleanses himself from the latter [from being a vessel of dishonor], he will be a vessel for honor, sanctified and useful for the Master, prepared for every good work" (explanation added). In other words, when you and I make conscious decisions to reflect Christ by allowing Him to work in our hearts, we are transformed into vessels of honor!

I can attest to this truth. When I became a Christian, I was a lot like the trashcan—full of negativity, judgments, and fears. None of these words described my righteousness in Christ. Little by little however, I made adjustments to my behavior (acting from the inside out) by allowing God's Word to change me. One decision at a time, I was transformed more and more into His image.

Have I arrived yet? No, of course not. But accepting God's love and forgiveness of my sins and then in turn, forgiving myself, accepting who He has made me to be and making righteous decisions for good and not evil, I am now a vessel that shines brighter and brighter, reflecting my Savior.

What's Your Value?

The real clincher to my transformation however, was when I realized God saw me with value whether I was like the trashcan or the vase. Let me ask this question: If I offered you a $100 bill, would you take it? Of course you would. Why? Because it has value. But what if I took that same $100 bill and wadded it up, threw it down, stepped on it, ground it into the dirt to the point it had minor tears in it, would you still take it? Yes! Because regardless of its condition, it still has value.

This is true of you and me in the eyes of God. No matter our condition, He sees us with value. He sees our potential and better than that, He sees Christ in us! This fact alone makes us of infinite worth to God.

This is why the Bible says the reflection of a believer in their mirror reflects the glory of the Lord. It is Christ in you. "But we all, with unveiled face, **beholding as in a mirror the glory of the Lord,** are being transformed into the same image from glory to glory, just as by the Spirit of the Lord" (2 Corinthians 3:18, emphasis added). From glory to glory, from faith to faith, from one revelation to another, God transforms us into His image by His Spirit. Our value is not lost based on performance. Our usefulness might be, but never our value.

What do I mean by that? It would be silly for me to put roses in my trashcan and set it out in my entryway to greet guests. In the same way, God recognizes that how we reflect Him draws others to Him or pushes them away. If God had made me a national speaker when I was a young Christian, I would've been a horrible representative! I had a potty-mouth, I was a complainer, I was ignorant of God's love, barely able to accept it for myself, and so on. But from one degree of glory to another, He has changed me into a vessel that reflects Him more accurately.

What Do You See?

I read a story about a man whose grandmother would position him in front of the mirror when he was a child. She would stand there degrading him, telling him what she thought about him. As a result, he grew up to hate mirrors. He avoided them at all cost. They were only a reminder of the pain inflicted on him as a child.

Ironically, when his grandmother died, he received her antique mirror as a part of her last will and testament. This infuriated him, and he considered throwing it away but decided instead to put it in the attic as if to imprison the awful mirror. This man never came to terms with his reflection. He was unable to see the glory of the Lord (God's potential within him) reflecting back. Instead, his reflection only duplicated the bitterness of his own soul.

Mirrors give faithful reflections. When you stand before a mirror and wave, the reflection waves. When you smile, it smiles. If you are bitter, it is bitter. If you feel inferior to it, it feels inferior to you.

But if you see Christ in your mirror, it will reflect Christ back to you. If you see hope, love, and acceptance, your mirror will reflect back to you what you see. "So all of us who have had that veil removed can see and reflect the glory of the Lord. And the Lord—who is the Spirit—makes us more and more like Him as we are changed into His glorious image" (2 Corinthians 3:18, NLT).

CHAPTER FOURTEEN

Awakening

*No single event can awaken within us a stranger totally
unknown to us. To live is to be slowly born.*

-Antoine de Saint-Exupery

In 1969, a doctor went to work at a facility that dealt with
patients who had long-term chronic and extremely debili-
tating diseases. This particular doctor was assigned to victims
of an encephalitis epidemic, which had left them in a catatonic
state. Once vibrant, they were now no longer able to do anything for themselves. With their arms and hands in crimped
positions, they simply gazed into space all day. When spoken
to, they were unable to respond. However, quite by accident,
the doctor discovered one of his patients had a surprising reflex.
When he threw a baseball towards her from across the room,
her crimped arm would reach out spontaneously and catch the
ball, though she otherwise continued to appear non-responsive.

To make a long story short, the doctor began performing
a variety of tests on his patients to find out if they were awake

on the inside, although they appeared catatonic on the outside. That summer, the doctor administered doses of an experimental drug to all of his patients and miraculously, they all awakened. Some of them had been in a semi-unconscious condition for 25 to 30 years, but now they were talking, walking, and interacting with others. It was truly amazing.

Unfortunately, their awakening didn't last. The medicine had only a short-term effect on the patients, and after a few months, they all returned to their lifeless state for no known reason. In the end, the doctor determined that although he had no understanding as to what helped or didn't help, he knew one thing for sure: Every human being has an inner person who needs to be awakened regardless of what we can see on the outside.[1] Is this not also true of our spiritual lives? Paul once said, "Awake to righteousness" (1 Corinthians 15:34).

Before receiving Christ and salvation, all human beings are physically alive yet spiritually catatonic. However, when the Spirit of the living God makes His home within the heart of a believer, there is a great awakening. "If anyone is in Christ, he is a new creation" (2 Corinthians 5:17). Physically, we may look the same on the day of our salvation as we did the day before, but we are not the same. And over time, that which has come alive on the inside begins to show itself on the outside.

I am not the same person today that I was before being born again. In fact, if I ever tell stories of my past, most people have a hard time believing me because the stories describe a person who is much different than who I am now.

Gail Sheehy once said, "If every day is an awakening, you will never grow old. You will just keep growing." This is how it is with our salvation. When our spirit man is born again (awakened to new life), every day becomes an opportunity to grow in Christ. Every day can be an awakening. When God set me in front of my mirror and said, "Now you tell her you love her and you forgive her," a darkened area of my heart was awakened to truth.

I believe this principle was an underlying meaning to Paul's words to the church in Rome when he said, "You know what [a critical] hour this is, how it is high time now for you to wake up out of your sleep (rouse to reality). For salvation (final deliverance) is nearer to us now than when we first believed (adhered to, trusted in, and relied on Christ, the Messiah)" (Romans 13:11, AMP). He wasn't speaking of awaking from literal sleep. Paul was referring to the catatonic state we once walked in before Christ and the danger of falling back into a similar condition.

> *Every issue, belief, attitude, or assumption is precisely the issue that stands between you and your relationships; and between you and yourself.*
> *-Author Unknown*

Salvation is not a one-time event in a person's life. It may have begun on a certain day, but it is a journey. Salvation is deliverance, safety, preservation, healing, and soundness of mind. Each of us need these provisions on a daily basis, not just one time at its introduction.

This is why it is so very important for us to awaken to righteousness! As you've been learning in this book, righteousness is both a position and an action. It is first our right standing with God, including our ability to stand before Him without guilt or inferiority as if we had never sinned, and then righteousness is our response to God's grace. It is the daily fruit we bear in our lives as we remember "whatever you do in word or deed, do all in the name of the Lord Jesus, giving thanks to God the Father through Him" (Colossians 3:17).

Jesus said, "Let your light so shine before men, that they may see your good works and glorify your Father in heaven" (Matthew 5:16). We are living in a critical hour. We don't know when our Savior will return for His Church, we only know it is one day closer today than it was yesterday. It is nearer to us now than when we first believed. The Scriptures encourage us to awaken (and stay awake) to righteousness because "In the way of righteousness is life, and in its pathway there is no death" (Proverbs 12:28).

Carl Gustav Jung said, "Your vision will become clear only when you can look into your heart. Who looks outside, dreams; who looks inside, awakes." Christ dwells within us! The very thought should cause our hearts to leap with inexpressible joy. An understanding of righteousness should be our motivation every day to remain awake in the midst of a dark world. Jesus gave us this warning: "Are there not twelve hours in the day? Anyone who walks about in the daytime does not stumble, because he sees [by] the light of this world. But if anyone walks about in the night, he stumbles, because there is no light in him [the light is lacking to him]" (John 11:9-10, AMP).

We have been awakened by the true light. Jesus is life, and His life is the light of men (John 1:4). The world around us is dark, and we are often tempted to sleep instead of shining our light in the darkness. But we have been awakened, and there is reason to rejoice.

How Fortunate We Are

What a God we have! And how fortunate we are to have him, this Father of our Master Jesus! Because Jesus was raised from the dead, we've been given a brand-new life and have everything to live for, including a future in heaven—and the future starts now! God is keeping careful watch over us and the future. The Day is coming when you'll have it all—life healed and whole. I know how great this makes you feel, even though you have to put up with every kind of aggravation in the meantime. Pure gold put in the fire comes out of it proved pure; genuine faith put through this suffering comes out proved genuine. When Jesus wraps this all up, it's your faith, not your gold, that God will have on display as evidence of His victory. You never saw him, yet you love him. You still don't see him, yet you trust him—with laughter and singing. Because you kept on believing, you'll get what you're looking forward to: total salvation.

1 Peter 1:3-9, MSG

How fortunate we are! Did you know the dictionary defines the word "fortunate" as lucky? I'm pretty confident the Apostle Peter wasn't referring to luck. Lucky describes something that happens by chance or by accident, not intentional. The patients in my earlier story did not awaken by luck. The doctor was intentionally trying to cure them. He was fortunate to have found something that worked—however brief that cure might have been.

In the same way, the life we have been given through salvation is anything but lucky! It was definitely intentional on God's part. This is why Peter rejoiced in saying, "What a God we have!"

We, who have received Jesus as our Lord and Savior, are most fortunate! Synonyms for *fortunate* include blessed, encouraged, favored, happy, promising, rosy, triumphant, victorious, well-off, and well-to-do. Why are we blessed? Why are we encouraged and happy? Why are we favored, rosy, and triumphant? Because we have been given a brand-new life in Christ Jesus! And this life is now a life worth living!

Not only that, but this life is never going to end. Eternal life is a quality of life that started at salvation but never ends. We don't have to sing "In the Sweet By and By" while we wait for this miserable life to end and heaven to receive and rescue us. No! Eternity has been placed in our hearts by the power of the Living God, who gave up His only begotten Son so that we may have life and life more abundantly.

Is heaven going to be wonderful? You bet! We can only imagine what it will truly be like. I have had some times with God where I was just swept away in the revelation of His goodness; times where I was literally overwhelmed with such joy that it felt like my heart might just burst. I think heaven will be like that and more. No wonder those who have tasted heaven early chose to stay rather than return to earth. As the Apostle Paul said, "For me, to live is Christ, and to die is gain" (Philippians 1:21). There is a day coming when we will have it all. But for now, to truly live is Christ, and for that we are most fortunate.

Remain Solid

My challenge to you now is this: Whatever you believe, believe it with all your heart. In James chapter 1, a double-minded person is compared to waves of the sea, that are blown and tossed by the wind. This is such a true picture of the inconsistent. One minute they seem strong in their conviction, but with a little peer pressure or persuasion, they flip and change like a pancake in a skillet. James said, "People who 'worry their prayers' are like wind-whipped waves. Don't think you're going to get anything from the Master that way, adrift at sea, keeping all your options open" (James 1:6-8, MSG). Isn't that what we're doing when we aren't firm in our belief system? We're really just "keeping all our options open," just in case.

Just in case what? Just in case God isn't who He says He is? Just in case God's Word is a lie and not the truth? Just in case it's more popular to be quiet about your faith and freedom in Christ? Or just in case it's politically correct to "go with the flow," letting others dictate your identity? What pleases God is your faith, not your changing belief system.

So I'm challenging you to decide: Are you the righteousness of God in Christ, or not?

It's good to have a teachable spirit, being humble before God and not pretending to know it all. But what do you believe? Are you solid in it? Or are you on the fence waiting for a strong wind to push you one way or the other? It'd be nice if you could guarantee the strong wind was a strong faith friend who'd push you in the right direction. But in your ignorance and lack of decision, you might be pushed in the wrong direction by a loud friend (not necessarily a smart one). "That's why Jesus lived and died and then lived again: so that He could be our Master across the entire range of life and death, and free us from the petty tyrannies of each other" (Romans 14:9, MSG).

You Believe This Stuff!

As I travel and speak on the topic of righteousness, I am often introduced to new people and places. During a particular weekend retreat, my message of righteousness also took on a flair of faith and believing. Sometimes, it's not enough to only teach on this subject. I often feel compelled to also challenge people to believe the message of righteousness because religion has made it out to seem pious or unattainable.

After my third session, a precious, elderly woman in her seventies approached me and said, "You know what makes you so good?" [Now pause for a second, and think about how you would answer that!] While I considered what she just said, she looked me square in the eyes and said, "Because you believe this stuff!" I laughed and responded, "Why, yes ma'am, I do! And so should you!"

Sadly, she explained that she had listened to many teachers over the years, but didn't always think they believed God's Word. I sympathized because at one time, I didn't either. My feelings and the thoughts in my head were often in complete opposition to God's Word. I dare say this is true of everyone.

But let's try looking at things through an eternal perspective. I remember hearing a story about a lady who was upset with her husband because he loved old western movies. She wanted him to get up and do something constructive instead of just sitting in front of the TV. As she was folding clothes in the other room, fuming about how relaxed he was in his chair, the Holy Spirit said to her, "And what does this have to do with eternity?" The obvious answer was: not much.

There's a lesson there for us. Instead of getting all upset about what others believe, why don't we make sure we're solid in what we believe? "Cultivate your own relationship with God, but don't impose it on others. You're fortunate if your behavior and your belief are coherent (harmonious). But if you're not sure, if you notice that you are acting in ways inconsistent with what you believe... then you know that you're out of line. If the way you live isn't consistent with what you believe, then it's wrong" (Romans 14:22-23, MSG, explanation added).

Although you and I are guaranteed to have days when we struggle, make mistakes, and simply dislike ourselves, it doesn't change God's Word. He has declared us to be the righteousness of God in Him despite our shortcomings. The Bible says, "The Kingdom of God is not a matter of what we eat or drink, but of living a life of goodness and peace and joy in the Holy Spirit. If you serve Christ with this attitude, you will please God, and others will approve of you, too" (Romans 14:17-18, NLT). Pleasing God with your faith starts with righteousness, your simple faith in Christ for the forgiveness of sins. Then it's a chain reaction from righteousness to peace to joy! If you're lacking peace and joy, you can be sure there's a snag in your belief system regarding righteousness.

It's normal for human beings to struggle with the balance between natural and spiritual principles. This is why God outlined His truth in His Word and then gave us the testimonies of others to encourage us along the way. For example, the Apostle Paul had experiences with God that could not be explained in the natural, so he described them this way: "I know a man in Christ who fourteen years ago—whether in the body I do not know, or whether out of the body I do not know, God knows—such a one was caught up to the third heaven. And I know such a man—whether in the body or out of the body I do not know, God knows—how he was caught up into Paradise and heard inexpressible words, which it is not lawful for a man to utter. Of such a one I will boast" (2 Corinthians 12:2-5). Who was this man he was referring to? Theologians all agree it was himself. Paul was referring to who he was in Christ. In an endeavor to describe his experiences with God, he was so caught up in the revelation of who God was and who he was in Him, that he wasn't even sure if it was an in- or out-of-body experience. He just knew it wasn't him, the mortal man; it was him, the man in Christ.

But there is a natural side too. Peter rejoiced over how fortunate we are to be saved, yet he said, "I know how great this makes you feel, even though you have to put up with every kind of aggravation in the meantime" (1 Peter 1:6, MSG). How true is that? No matter how much I learn about this life in Christ and the righteousness we have received through Him, there are still days I am tempted to pull my hair out. Obviously I don't because of what I have learned about our life in Christ. As Peter explained, "Pure gold put in the fire comes out proved pure; genuine faith put through this suffering [this occasional aggravation] comes out proved genuine" (1 Peter 1:7, MSG, explanation added). Why? Because in all things we have the victory in Christ Jesus. There really is nothing to lose; only everything to gain!

Let me repeat Paul's words: *"For me, to live is Christ, and to die is gain!"* Sounds like a win-win situation to me. How about to you?

Do you believe this way?

Are you convinced yet?

If you love Jesus, your answer should be yes. It's true you may still be growing in this revelation, but the Holy Spirit is always ready to reveal these truths to you. Think about it, you never saw Him, yet you loved Him. You still don't see Him, yet you trust Him. Don't you think there's more to the package of this life in Christ than what you know right now? It doesn't matter who we are or where we are in our walk with God, as Christians, there is always more to learn, more to be revealed, and more to experience! How fortunate we really are!

The goal is to keep on believing! Sure, for a little while we may be grieved by various trials (1 Peter 1:6), but that isn't cause to quit believing. On the contrary, it is all the more reason to keep believing. Lean on God's faithfulness. Remember, "If we are faithless, He remains faithful; He cannot deny Himself" (2 Timothy 2:13). The result of your continued faith in God? Total salvation! The word *total* means whole, entire, full-blown, full-scale, undisputed, unlimited, and thorough!

This is your salvation. This is the life we now live in Christ, and the fullness of it is still being revealed. How fortunate

(blessed, encouraged, favored, happy, promising, rosy, triumphant, victorious, well-off, and well-to-do) you and I are as the
righteousness of God in Christ!

CHAPTER FIFTEEN

Living Out Our Righteousness

A little knowledge that acts is worth infinitely more than much knowledge that is idle.

-Kahill Gibran

People have asked me, "Daphne, why do you talk so much about righteousness?"

For starters, the word "righteousness" is mentioned 292 times in the *New King James Bible* alone. This makes me think it might be important to God. And secondly, my understanding of righteousness has been so much more than mere head knowledge. I now have a faith I live by, a purpose I live for, and (thanks to the message of righteousness) a self I can live with.

I don't want to keep this good news to myself any more than the Apostle Paul wanted to keep his revelation to himself. In Philippians 3:1, he said, "My brethren, rejoice in the Lord. For me to write the same things to you is not tedious, but for you it is safe." The New Living translation reads, "I never get tired of telling you these things, and I do it to safeguard your faith." The *New Century Version* puts it this way, "It is no trouble for me to write the same things to you again, and it will help you be more ready." This is my primary reason for speaking so often of righteousness—that it will help those who hear.

I have come to realize: A faith to live by and a purpose to live for are of no matter if you don't have a self you can live with.

You are not the affliction. You are not the disease. Jesus came to change all that. "For He made Him who knew no sin to be sin for us, that we might become the righteousness of God in Him" (2 Corinthians 5:21).

Step One

Throughout this book, I've repeatedly shared with you how the Holy Spirit prompted me to say something. I was slow to realize the power of my own voice. The objective of the Holy Spirit was to teach me how to see myself differently by changing the way I thought. Through my own confession—saying aloud what God had already said of me in His Word—my self-image began to change in proportion to what I was saying.

It wasn't enough to simply know that there is no condemnation for those who are in Christ Jesus or that I'm the righteousness of God in Christ; I was only able to embrace these truths because the Holy Spirit had me continually confess them. Second Corinthians 4:13 states: "And since we have the same spirit of faith, according to what is written, 'I believed and therefore I spoke,' we also believe and therefore speak." It is very important for you to speak your faith. You won't always feel forgiven or righteous (much less worthy of such), but regardless, you must learn to confess God's Word in faith, believing it is true. This is step one.

Hebrews 11:1-3 says, "Faith is the substance of things hoped for, the evidence of things not seen. For by it the elders obtained a good testimony. By faith we understand that the worlds were framed by the word of God, so that the things which are seen were not made of things which are visible." In other words, the world was created by the word of God. We see in Genesis that God "spoke" and "it was," so although God's word was not "seen," it was creative in power.

As children of God, we have been given the same ability to create with our words. This is why the writer of Hebrews said, "by [faith] the elders obtained a good testimony" referring to the prophets (those who came before Christ). They had a spirit of faith, and we have the same spirit of faith. By biblical definition, a spirit of faith describes what we are doing with what we believe. The Apostle Paul said, "I believe and therefore I speak."

The problem is most of us haven't understood the power of speaking our faith. We were taught that to have faith, we must believe in Christ; but we've forgotten that we had to confess Him also. How we began in faith is how we must continue in faith—through our believing and speaking.

Since this is foreign to most of us who have always had a quiet faith, we have to be trained. This is exactly what the Holy Spirit did in my life. I didn't always believe the confessions He was having me make, but the Holy Spirit knew my spirit would be transformed nonetheless. Thankfully, we have the disciples of Jesus as another example of this. They too, had to be schooled into a spirit of faith.

Faith School

We find our lesson in Mark 11:22-23, when Jesus explained to His disciples how to operate in faith. After passing by a fig tree Jesus had cursed the day before, the disciples saw it had withered up and were amazed, so they questioned Him about it. Mark Hankins says, "Jesus could have told His disciples, 'Now this is a deity trick that only Me, God, and the Holy Spirit know how to do, so don't try this at home.'" But that's not what Jesus said.

On the contrary, He told them, "Have faith in God" (Mark 11:22). If, by this statement, Jesus meant for us to only believe God, His following words would've been something like: "God is faithful and trustworthy, therefore have faith in Him." But instead, Jesus continued by telling His disciples (and us) how to have faith. In other words, Jesus was really telling them, "Have the God-kind of faith."

What is the God-kind of faith? Well, for starters, God spoke, and it was. Doing the same, Jesus spoke to the fig tree, and it changed. Even Abraham changed his circumstances through his confession. Paul said Abraham exercised the God-kind of faith when, "contrary to [natural] hope in [spiritual] hope [he] believed, so that he became the father of many nations, according to what was spoken" (Romans 4:18, explanation added). In other words, despite how he felt or what it looked like, Abraham said what God said. He called himself the father of many nations as if he had many descendants, even though he did not yet have any children. He declared what was going to be, not necessarily what was at the moment. Faith is believing and speaking. It's not enough for you and I to just believe.

Jesus said, "For assuredly, I tell you, whoever says to this mountain, 'Be removed and be cast into the sea,' and does not doubt in his heart, but **believes** that those things he says will be done, he will have whatever he says" (Mark 11:23, emphasis added). Did you notice the emphasis Jesus put on what we say? He mentioned saying three times and believing only once. This is why you and I can school ourselves into faith. The formula Jesus gave us is 3:1—for every three times you speak your faith, your believing will increase by one.

Most of the time, when people are in a pressure situation, they zip their lips and say nothing because Momma always said, "If you can't say something nice, don't say anything at all!" But Momma's instructions weren't meant to be applied to speaking our faith. In that case, we need to do just the opposite.

So our formula is: 3 parts say = 1 part belief

Faith is believing and speaking. Therefore, to increase your believing (or your faith), you must speak.

Revelation

As I was learning and meditating on this myself, the Holy Spirit showed me an example of a post office. When I lived out in the country, my mail and packages had to be picked up at our local post office. In Romans 10:17, the Bible says, "Faith comes by hearing, and hearing by the Word." And we've already read,

"Faith is the substance of things hoped for" (Hebrews 11:1). The Holy Spirit said to me: "Hearing the Word of God is an example of how faith comes [just like your packages that arrive at the post office]. But faith is received when you actually take them home and open them." In other words, people receive what they need (such as letters of promise and packages of inheritance) as they study and get revelation of God's Word. But then just like the person who tossed a letter on the table, not realizing it contained something valuable, we too can leave our promises unopened, never fully receiving what God has given to us. Opening our mouths and speaking aloud what God has said of us in His Word is how we unseal His promises for ourselves. If we are struggling with believing God's promises, it is also how we school ourselves into faith.

Webster's Dictionary defines *faith* as "a firm belief in something for which there is no proof."[1] This is a good definition, but it also explains why people are weak in faith. If faith is a firm belief or persuasion and a person is not yet firmly persuaded, then what? Then we need to go back to Jesus' instruction in Mark 11:23 and do a whole lot more saying! Remember our formula: 3 parts say = 1 part belief.

This is why the Word of God in your mouth is so powerful, while the Word of God on your shelf isn't. Until someone speaks it, it just lies dormant.

Locate Your Faith

Another word we need to understand is perception. *Webster's* defines *perception* as "to become aware of through the senses, and especially through sight."[2] This is where people get snagged. We are guilty of building our faith on our senses or sight instead of on what God has said in His Word.

Up until now, I dare say you have predominantly lived by perception (or your senses). All of us have! We learned at an early age to live by what we see, feel, hear, and smell. This isn't entirely wrong, but it's not how you operate in a spirit of faith. The Bible says, "For we walk by faith, not by sight" (2 Corinthians 5:7). Yet most do just the opposite, which might explain why the enemy has been able to take such advantage of us.

Remember that faith is the substance of things hoped for, the evidence of things not seen. There are two parts to our faith:

- <u>Part one is believing</u>: it is the substance, or raw material, we give God to work with.
- <u>Part two is speaking</u>: it is the evidence of things not seen. These are our words.

Words can be heard but not seen. This is why if you and I spent a little time together, I would know fairly quickly where your faith is simply by listening to you. Matthew 12:34 says, "Out of the abundance of the heart the mouth speaks."

If you want to grow in faith and walk in the promises of God, you must have both parts. Even if you start with no belief, you can build faith by speaking. Never in the Word of God does it say, "If you just believe and say nothing, you'll have what you believe."

Faith in Action

Let me give you an example of faith in action. Hebrews, chapter 11 is known as the "Faith Hall of Fame." It is a record of men and women who activated their faith, received their promises, and pleased God in the process. For the sake of example, in each of these passages I'm going to replace the word "faith" with the words "believing and speaking" to illustrate how a spirit of faith works.

- By believing and speaking, Abel obtained a good testimony (verse 4).
- By believing and speaking, Enoch pleased God (verse 5).
- By believing and speaking, Abraham obeyed when he was called to go out (verse 8).
- By believing and speaking, Sarah herself received strength to conceive (verse 11).
- By believing and speaking, Moses forsook Egypt, not fearing the wrath of the king; for he endured as seeing Him who is invisible (verse 27).
- By believing and speaking, the harlot Rahab did not perish with those who did not believe, when she had received the spies with peace (verse 31).

Pause for a moment.

This is the Faith Hall of Fame. Did the scriptures have to call Rahab a harlot? Couldn't it have simply said she was a woman who pleased God when she helped the spies? No, because at the time she was a harlot. Yet in God's eyes, her past was not an indicator of her future. The same is true for you and me! In other words, by faith (by believing and speaking) our current situation can change.

Never get caught up in labels. Jesus said we would have what we say, not what others say (Mark 11:23).

Hebrews 11:32-34 continues: "And what more shall I say? For the time would fail me to tell of Gideon and Barak and Samson and Jephthah, also of David and Samuel and the prophets: who through faith [believing and speaking] subdued kingdoms, worked righteousness, obtained promises, stopped the mouths of lions, quenched the violence of fire, escaped the edge of the sword, out of weakness were made strong, became valiant in battle, and turned to flight the armies of the aliens." These men and women did amazing feats through faith. But don't forget, it wasn't by believing only. They also spoke what they believed, and God met them at their confession.

> *All the art of living lies in a fine mingling of letting go and holding on.*
> *-Havelock Ellis*

So What Now?

As a believer in Christ, you have been declared righteous and acceptable before God. You have been given the ability to stand before Him without guilt or inferiority as if you had never sinned. It is not something you are working towards. This gift was given to you when you were born again.

I know you've blown it more than once since the day of salvation; so have I. So what now? Just because you have begun to understand who you are in Christ and that your performance is not getting you any closer to righteousness than you already were, do you now have the freedom to do whatever you want? No, sin is sin, and it's nothing to laugh at or take lightly. But because we can all fall into sin at one time or another, we need to remember its effect.

A minister once said 1 John 1:9 is the Christian's "bar of soap": "If we confess our sins, He is faithful and just to forgive us our sins and to cleanse us from all unrighteousness." So let me ask you a question: If all the unrighteousness is cleansed when we confess our sins, what is left? Righteousness.

On your first day of salvation, you prayed and accepted Jesus as your Lord and Savior. You were then cleansed, given a clean slate, and declared righteous before God. So now also, when you confess your sins to God, you can lift your head from prayer just as you did on the very first day and accept your right standing with Him. He said in Isaiah 43:25, "I—yes, I alone— will blot out your sins for my own sake and will never think of them again" (NLT). God is not keeping a record of your for- given sins, and neither should you.

Remember, "There is therefore now no condemnation for those who are in Christ Jesus" (Romans 8:1). This very minute, if you slip up and blow it, you can immediately ask for forgiveness and move forward without guilt or condemnation. Every day is a new day, and every minute is a new minute. When you confess and repent, God forgives and forgets and puts you back in right standing with Him. You are re-established in righteousness.

But it doesn't end there. You will have to pursue these things because the devil wants to rob you of your knowledge of who you are in Christ and the blessings you've freely received.

First Timothy 6:11-12 says, "But you, O man of God, flee these [immoral] things and **pursue righteousness**, godliness, faith, love, patience, gentleness. Fight the good fight of faith, lay hold on eternal life, to which you were also called and have confessed the good confession in the presence of many witnesses" (emphasis and explanation added).

You must pursue righteousness. You can't earn it, but you can guard and protect it by setting your mind on the things of God and not the things of your flesh. Be prepared, it is a fight. You still have a flesh nature that wants to contradict what you now know to be true. You must fight the good fight of faith because your feelings will always try to dictate your faith (and it's a fight)!

Paul said to "lay hold on eternal life." It's not enough to know you will live forever in heaven with God. You must lay hold, grasp, take for yourself the eternal life and quality of life Jesus purchased for you. This is only accomplished by renewing your mind daily in God's Word. Jeremiah 29:11 says God has a plan for every believer. "For I know the thoughts that I think toward you, says the Lord, thoughts of peace and not of evil, to give you a future and a hope." But we are responsible for getting into His Word and finding out for ourselves what those thoughts and plans are. The devil would like nothing more than to block or water down our understanding of righteousness.

Deep Roots Are Strong

The Bible has scripture after scripture referring to the "righteous" and every one of them is talking about those who have put their faith in Christ. For example, Psalm 92:12 says, "The righteous shall flourish like a palm tree." Have you ever noticed how palm trees are the only things still standing after a hurri-cane has ripped through a city? This is

> *Those who danced were thought to be quite insane by those who could not hear the music.*
> *-Angela Monet*

because they have strong, deep roots. The Bible says the righteous, refer-ring to you and I, will flourish like the palm tree. In other words, when you push down deep and establish your roots in the knowledge of who you are in Christ, the devil will never win—no matter how hard a storm he blows your way.

Satan would love to keep you feeling insecure by mak-ing you think God has abandoned you in the storm, but don't believe it. Instead, put your faith in God's promises, and hold on! Believe God's Word, and keep speaking it!

Act on Your Knowledge

But that's not all. Knowledge isn't enough; you must act on it. "But be doers of the word and not hearers only, deceiving your-selves. For if anyone is a hearer of the Word and not a doer, he is like a man observing his natural face in a mirror; for he observes himself, goes away, and immediately forgets what kind of man he was" (James 1:22-24).

Take a closer look into the perfect law of liberty—God's Word. Let it be your mirror.

"He who looks into the perfect law of liberty and continues in it, and is not a forgetful hearer but a doer of the work, this one will be blessed in what he does" (James 1:25).

I still blow it at times, and it's tempting to stay disappointed in myself. But I refuse to let guilt and condemnation rule my life anymore, and neither should you. Whether your feelings match what you know or not, determine to believe God's Word and act on it. Then hold your head high with the revelation He has forgiven you and therefore, your righteousness is intact.

Exercise Your Faith

Going back to speaking our faith, Mark Brazee has a wonderful illustration on this subject. He says, "Faith is like a muscle. Think back on a time when you physically exerted yourself, such as in yard work or exercise, and you found a muscle you hadn't used for awhile. Maybe it hurt for two or three days, having become weak from lack of use. If you start using that forgotten muscle every day, it will actually grow in size and strength.

"However, if you let it lie dormant, then the next time you use it, you'll have to pump it up and get it working all over again. In the same manner, our capacity to operate in faith comes from hearing the Word of God, but our faith doesn't grow because we hear. We can feed and feed and feed a muscle, but it only grows in strength as we exercise it. Faith is the same way." [3]

You can use your faith (through your confession) to push insecurities and doubts away just like a weightlifter uses weights. Every time he pushes the weights away, he gains a little more strength. In the same way, every time you push the lies of the enemy away, you grow stronger.

Don't Lose What You've Gained

Jesus said in John 10:10, "The thief does not come except to steal, and to kill, and to destroy. I have come that they may have life, and that they may have it more abundantly." Remember, the devil's main purpose in this world is to kill your enthusiasm, steal your joy, and destroy your purpose. In order to fight off the enemy and his plan to rob you of the freedom you have in Christ, you must never pick up the old, dead man of sin and condemnation again. If you're not careful, you will naturally pick up old habits and lose what you've gained.

When I was pregnant with our second child, Christopher, he was breach. After months of waiting for him to turn, the doctors decided to turn him for me so I could have a natural delivery and avoid a c-section. I was told that as soon as they turned him in my womb, they would immediately begin to induce labor. The doctors explained that if they allowed me to go home and wait for my body to begin labor on its own, the baby would flip back around to his original position because although it was dangerous, it was what he was accustomed to and where he was comfortable. In the same way, if you don't act on the truths you've learned in this book and begin to renew your mind to them immediately, you will naturally flip back to your original position, even though it means bondage and danger for you.

Press Toward the Goal

It's now time to live out your righteousness! You are the righteousness of God in Christ Jesus! So face your mirror without condemnation. Pursue righteousness. Make a choice to serve God and not the flesh. Fight the good fight. And always press toward the goal.

As Paul summarized his understanding of who he was in Christ in Philippians 3:9-10, 13-14, let this be your confession also:

> May I be found in Him, not having my own righteousness, which is from the law, but that which is through faith in Christ, the righteousness which is from God by faith; that I may know Him and the power of His resurrection. Though I am still not all I should be, I am focusing all my energies on this one thing: Forgetting the past and looking forward to what lies ahead, I strain to reach the end of the race and receive the prize for which God, through Christ Jesus, is calling us up to Heaven.

WORKBOOK

To all the people who lived in the dark,
yet longed for the light; who knew there was more,
but lived with much less; who smiled on the outside
to cover the pain; who wanted to believe,
but needed a guide.

INTRODUCTION TO THE WORKBOOK

"Greatness is not where we stand, but in what direction we are moving. We must sail sometimes with the wind and sometimes against it—but sail we must and not drift, nor lie at anchor."

-Oliver Wendell Holmes

How true! As much as we would love the wind to be at our back all the time, pushing us forward with ease, life is not guaranteed to be that easy. The problem lies within what we do when the wind is against us. Too often, people quit pressing forward and just drift along hoping a new tailwind will come, or they put an anchor down and stop altogether. Both are foolish without clear direction from God.

You may remember the Apostle Paul's voyage to Rome. In Acts, Chapter 27, we find him as a prisoner on a boat sailing along the coasts. A great storm had arisen and the winds became contrary and increasingly more difficult to navigate through. Paul fasted and prayed for a time and then addressed those in charge saying, *"Men, I perceive that this voyage will end with disaster and much loss, not only of the cargo and ship, but also our lives"* (Acts 27:10).

There's a lesson here for us: When opposition arises suddenly, the first thing we must do is seek God. And secondly, we must heed what He says.

Paul's voyage was out of his control, but because he continued to seek God there was no loss of life—only material things. Yet Paul and his shipmates encountered that loss because God's Word wasn't heeded fully. Let this be an example for us. Our adversity could end in destruction as well if we lightly esteem seeking God, or worse, don't heed His instructions at all.

Opposition however, in and of itself, is not always a sign to stop or quit. When Peter walked on the water, the winds were quite boisterous. Yet, Jesus said to Peter, *"Come."* Jesus didn't say, *"No Peter, it's too dangerous."* On the contrary, He only scolded him for his lack of faith. Instead of continuing in God's Word, Peter set his eyes on the effects of the wind and sank.

Oliver Wendell Holmes said it well: "Greatness is not where we stand, but in what direction we are moving." If we only judge our situation by what it looks like, we may miss a miracle. But God said, *"I will bring the blind by a way they did not know; I will lead them in paths they have not known. I will make darkness light before them, and crooked places straight. These things I will do for them, and not forsake them"* (Isaiah 42:16).

If you drift or put down anchor in fear of the crooked places, how do you know God wasn't about to make them straight and smooth for His glory? Or how do you know if the apparent darkness in front of you won't suddenly come to light as you step forward in faith? The Book of Revelation even speaks of the inheritance promised to OVERCOMERS. But how can we overcome if all we want is a tailwind?

There are many things in my life I have no desire whatsoever of re-living. But I can tell you this: I am better and stronger on this side of it and therefore grateful for what I've learned. Winds of opposition should push us further into God's Word for help. I know not every opposition I have faced was from God. Many were my own doing. But just as Jesus spoke to Peter, *"Come,"* in the midst of his storm, He will do the same for us when look to Him for help. Regardless of what we are facing, His Word will speak to us and tell us what to do.

But we must first allow ourselves to be vulnerable. Real help can only be given to those who are open and authentic with themselves and God.

As you study scripture, you will find numerous examples of God giving divine direction in the midst of apparent opposition. In Genesis 12:1, for example, Abraham faced family opposition and God instructed him to *"Leave your land, your relatives, and your father's home. Go to the land that I will show you."*

Abraham obeyed and pressed forward in his assignment. It's not easy to leave family and comfort to go into unknown territory, but if it's freedom you're seeking, God may be taking you on the path first to show others the way later.

For certain, you can't base things on what it looks like or how it feels. A tailwind—or lack of one—should never be an indicator of our assignment. Trusting the tailwind is too much like "walking by sight" and not by faith!

Psalm 119:105 says, *"Thy word is a lamp unto my feet, and a light unto my path."* Our cars would never leave the parking lot after dark if we didn't trust our headlights. In the same way, our lives are to be directed by the Word of God, which lights our path when it looks dark or crooked or opposing. To drift at sea or throw down an anchor because of fear only leaves you vulnerable to the power of the sea and its inhabitants.

But God has given us, as believers, authority to dominate opposing forces. The balance is in knowing when to sail forward and when to wait on the Lord. The Apostle Paul was right to wait and Peter was right to step out and walk on the water— *although both had opposing winds.* They each had different circumstances, yet they each knew the Lord intimately. So in both cases, it was their intimacy with God that led them. And it is your intimacy with God that will lead you!

I challenge you to be real and authentic with yourself and God as you work through this book. Don't skip questions or leave them blank. If you feel challenged, take a break, pray, and ask God why. Facing a hard question isn't a sign God wants you to stop; it's a sign God wants you to heal.

I've prayed for you and I know God will complete what He's begun.

God bless,
Daphne

INSTRUCTIONS

This workbook was designed to help you have an interactive approach to the truths found in *Facing the Mirror: Finding a Self to Live With*. Too often, readers relate to the author but never really look in their own heart. Instead, they gain head knowledge but little heart change. The goal of this workbook is to help you look within by challenging things such as:

- What is my belief system?
- Why do I think this way?
- How do I replace lies with truth?

The best way to use this material is to read one chapter at a time in the book, stopping at the end of each chapter to answer the questions here. At the end of each workbook chapter, you will also find a reference of scriptures used in the book chapters as a handy study guide for your own personal time with God and His Word.

Meditate on these. Allow the Holy Spirit to reveal more truth to you.

This workbook is perfect for both individual and group study. In a group setting, read the chapter and answer questions at home on your own first. Then gather and share thoughts as you're comfortable. Not everything has to be shared—but allow yourself to learn from and/or help others regarding the things you've come to realize about righteousness and who you are in Christ.

For questions, email: info@daphnedelay.com

WORKBOOK CHAPTER ONE

Through the Fire and Past the Mirror

1. Mirrors faithfully reflect whatever is placed in front of them. For that reason, people avoid them. *Do you?* Explain why or why not:

   _____

   _____

   _____

   _____

   _____

   _____

   _____

   _____

   _____

2. When you look in a mirror, you can simply look at your reflection, taking a quick glance at the exterior, or you can pause and look inside at the real person. A friend of mine

once said she never stayed in front of her mirror more than 30 seconds at a time because she despised her reflection. Describe your relationship with your mirror:

_____

_____

_____

_____

_____

_____

_____

_____

_____

TRUTH

Insecurity has the ability to squelch dreams, mask truth, and redefine destinies.

3. Adjectives are words used to *describe* a person, place or thing. Take a minute to look in your mirror and then write down five adjectives that describe the person looking back at you. Explain each one:

1. Adjective: _____

_____

_____

_____

_____

2. Adjective: _____

_____

_____

_____

_____

3. Adjective: _____

_____

_____

_____

_____

4. Adjective: _____

_____

_____

_____

_____

5. Adjective: _____

_____

_____

_____

_____

Take a Closer Look...

Based on what you've learned, reflect on these quotes from Chapter 1:

Love yourself, for if you don't, how can you expect anybody else to love you?—AUTHOR UNKNOWN

_____

_____

_____

_____

_____

Life is a mirror and will reflect back to the thinker what he thinks into it.—EARNEST HOLMES

_____

_____

_____

_____

_____

Study Scriptures: *Proverbs 23:7a, Romans 12:2, Philippians 4:7, Psalm 119:92, Romans 4:18, Psalm 27:13*

WORKBOOK CHAPTER TWO

"You Be (Like) Jesus"

1. Due to the shame I felt over my sins, I wrestled with feelings of separation from God, which were actually my doing, not His. If you've ever felt like there was a wall between you and God, explain:

   _____

   _____

   _____

   _____

   _____

2. Remember, our eyes are the windows to our soul. What are your eyes saying?

   _____

   _____

   _____

   _____

3. Would you say the "real" you is in hiding? Yes _____
   No _____ Maybe you've mastered the ability to look like
   you have it all together. Perhaps you've stopped looking
   at anything but the surface. Who is hidden under your
   exterior?

   _____

   _____

   _____

   _____

   _____

   _____

4. Many times we've built walls around us that keep God at
   a distance. If you can relate to the illustration of the "glass
   box," what are the *walls* holding you inside? Describe them:

   _____

   _____

   _____

   _____

   _____

   _____

5. All of us are guilty of holding ourselves in unforgiveness at
   one point or another. It may be over something recent, or it
   may be over one or more things that have happened in the
   past. In either case, describe the roots of unforgiveness in
   your heart:

_____

_____

_____

_____

_____

_____

TRUTH

Satan's best-laid plan is to have
us destroy ourselves first.

6. *Here's a very important question:* When did you make a decision to receive Jesus and accept Him as your Savior?

_____

_____

_____

_____

_____

Going to church and doing good things does not save a person. As we move on in this study, it will be very important for you to have accepted Jesus as *your* personal Savior in order to grasp the teachings of righteousness (which will be explained later). The Bible says, *"If you confess with your mouth the Lord Jesus and believe in your heart that God has raised Him from the dead, you will be saved"* (Romans 10:9). It's that simple.

If you need to, pray this prayer:

"Heavenly Father, I may not understand everything yet. But I recognize I am a sinner and I need a Savior. I believe Jesus is Your Son. I believe You raised Him from the dead. I believe He died for my sins. Therefore, I choose to confess Jesus as Lord of my life. Make my heart Your home. Amen."

If you just prayed that prayer, or if you prayed a similar prayer at one time, then make a mental note. Being saved is the beginning. Regardless if you have been a Christian for three minutes, three months or fifty-three years, it is important for you to know when your starting point began and how you felt at the time.

7. Take a moment and reflect on your feelings regarding salvation. What does it mean to you?

_____

_____

_____

_____

_____

Take a Closer Look...

Based on what you've learned, reflect on these quotes from Chapter 2:

The art of pleasing is the art of deception.—LUC DE CLAPIERS

_____

_____

_____

_____

_____

The greatest deception men suffer is from their own opinions.
—LEONARDO DA VINCI

_____

_____

_____

_____

Study Scriptures: *Genesis 1:26, Colossians 3:3, 2 Timothy 2:26, Romans 7:24, 2 Corinthians 5:17, Proverbs 27:19*

WORKBOOK CHAPTER THREE

Changing Clothes

1. A mold is something that gives shape to another thing. Do you have molds you have tried to fit into during your life? *Maybe family molds? Job molds? Identity molds?* If so, what were they? Explain them:

   _____

   _____

   _____

   _____

   _____

2. When a person gives their heart to Jesus, their inward man is drastically changed. Part of the struggle I felt was between my inward man who had been forgiven and the old sinful man who had never been laid to rest. If you can relate to this, describe your struggle:

   _____

   _____

_____

_____

_____

3. Can you imagine having to carry around a dead body every-where? There's no doubt it would determine where you went and what you did. Is there anything in your self-image that feels like that dead body? Explain:

_____

_____

_____

_____

_____

_____

TRUTH

Conviction is how God corrects us.
Condemnation is how the devil defeats us.

4. What steps can you take to cast off any negative self-image?

_____

_____

_____

_____

_____

5. It's so easy to get caught in the cycle of doing good, feeling unworthy, giving in to sin, feeling more unworthy, and so on and so forth. Somewhere in there we must break the cycle by renewing our mind to God's view of us. So, in looking back on your walk with God, can you relate to the feeling of "spiritually" running around naked? If yes, how?

_____

_____

_____

_____

_____

6. If you feel naked, what old habits do you tend to put on?

_____

_____

_____

_____

_____

7. Our relationship with God can be stunted because of unforgiveness. God has forgiven you of your sins. He's not mad at you. If you were to remind Him of a sin you committed before you were born-again, He wouldn't remember it. It has been forgiven and forgotten. The bottom line is: *Have you forgiven yourself?*

_____

_____

_____

_____

_____

What areas in your life still need forgiveness?

_____

_____

_____

_____

_____

TRUTH

**In order to break out of the vicious cycle
of guilt, shame, and inferiority, you need to make
a decision right now if you are going to believe
God's Word—not just part of it, but all of it.**

Take a Closer Look...

Based on what you've learned, reflect on these quotes from
Chapter 3:

*One reason God created time was so there would be a place to
bury the failures of the past.*—JAMES LONG

_____

_____

_____

_____

_____

All men are not cast in the same mold.—AUTHOR UNKNOWN

_____

_____

_____

_____

_____

Study Scriptures: *Romans 8:1, 2 Corinthians 5:21, 2 Corinthians 5:17, Ephesians 4:22-24, Isaiah 60:10, Romans 6:6*

WORKBOOK CHAPTER FOUR

Cricket Mentalities

1. *How we view ourselves will always have a greater impact on us than how we view God.* Really think about that... Do the feelings you have towards yourself override God's Word? Yes _____ No _____ Explain:

    _____

    _____

    _____

    _____

    _____

2. Have you placed yourself as judge and jury? If yes, then how?

    _____

    _____

    _____

    _____

    _____

TRUTH

God's people are destroyed because of ignorance; and in that condition, Satan takes advantage of us.

3. Satan is deceptive, but God has tried to warn us. The Message Bible says, *"My people are [destroyed] because they don't know what's right or true"* (Hosea 4:6). Does this, in any way, describe you? Explain:

_____

_____

_____

_____

_____

4. One side of the scale holds the knowledge of who we are *in* Christ. The other side holds the knowledge of who we are *without* Christ. The scale can tip in either direction. Which direction would you say your scale is tipping right now, and why?

_____

_____

_____

_____

_____

5. Your heart has boundaries, which have been placed there by the things you think and say. Be honest with yourself and examine the boundaries of your heart. Are they protecting you from the lies of the world by holding in God's good word? Or, are your boundaries built by negative experiences that have now become a thick wall? Explain:

_____

_____

_____

_____

_____

_____

_____

Take a Closer Look...

Based on what you've learned, reflect on these quotes from Chapter 4:

I don't think of all the misery but of all the beauty that still remains. —ANNE FRANK

_____

_____

_____

_____

_____

_____

It is what a man thinks of himself that really determines his fate.—HENRY DAVID THOREAU

_____

_____

_____

_____

_____

_____

_____

Study Scriptures: *Numbers 13:1-33, Matthew 12:34, Mark 11:23, Psalm 4:23, Proverbs 23:7a, Hosea 4:6, 2 Corinthians 2:11, Hebrews 10:17, Psalm 145:8, 1 Timothy 2:4*

WORKBOOK CHAPTER FIVE

The Truth About God

1. If God is good, then the devil is bad. They are complete opposites. Yet somehow, the devil has manipulated the church into believing God is the One who is hard, harsh, and unloving. Up until this point, what has your perception of God been?

    _____

    _____

    _____

    _____

    _____

2. It's natural to hear the word "Father" and compare God to our earthly dad. Describe the relationship (or lack of) you have had with your dad:

    _____

    _____

    _____

_____

_____

_____

3. Now in comparison, how has that relationship affected your
    view of God:

_____

_____

_____

_____

TRUTH

**Despite all my mistakes, I've yet to
hear God say, "Off with her head!"**

---

4. It's amazing to think back on our days *before Christ* and
    the unknown dangers He helped us avoid—even before we
    gave our hearts and lives to Him. Take a minute and recall
    some of the things He protected you from, or led you to, in
    order to help you finally find Him:

_____

_____

_____

_____

Take a Closer Look...

Based on what you've learned, reflect on these quotes from Chapter 5:

You can bend it and twist it... You can misuse and abuse it...
But even God cannot change the Truth. —MICHAEL LEVY

_____

_____

_____

_____

_____

Whenever you have truth it must be given with love,
or the message and the messenger will be rejected.
—MAHATMA GANDHI

_____

_____

_____

_____

_____

Study Scriptures: *Romans 2:4, Titus 3:3-5, Romans 5:8,*
Romans 3:24, Romans 11:6, 1 John 4:8, John 3:16, 1 Corinthians
13:4-7, 1 John 3:1, John 20:17, 1 John 4:19, 1 Peter 2:25,
Ezekiel 34:11-12, Isaiah 40:11, Psalm 71:2

WORKBOOK CHAPTER SIX

A Permanent Solution

1. Adam and Eve had an open, direct relationship with God. Disobedience introduced sin, which then separated them from God. Did you notice however, that God didn't have to tell them sin was the cause for their separation? They immediately knew. They were ashamed. Is sin causing you to feel ashamed? Yes _____ No _____ In what way might you be hiding from God?

   _____

   _____

   _____

   _____

   _____

2. The blood of animals was only a temporary solution to man's sin problem. Jesus however, *made peace (reconciliation) through the Blood of the Cross"* as the permanent solution. The significance of this began with the original

relationship God had with Adam and Eve. They spent time together talking openly without condemnation or insecurity. Do you believe God wants that kind of relationship with you? Explain why or why not:

_____

_____

_____

_____

_____

3. Describe your current relationship with God:

_____

_____

_____

_____

_____

4. Satan hasn't changed. He still uses the same deceptive bag of tricks he used on Adam and Eve. The problem is, deceived people aren't aware they're deceived unless God's Word reveals truth. What areas of deception are being exposed to you right now?

_____

_____

_____

_____

_____

TRUTH

It seems just as 2+2 = 4, righteousness is the sum of God's desire and God's direction for our lives.

5. What is having the greatest impact on you: Your view of God? Or your view of yourself? Explain:

_____

_____

_____

_____

_____

_____

TRUTH

Be warned: Satan is still up to his old tricks. He will use anything he can to deceive us, including insecurities, feelings of low self-worth, fears, failures, regrets and disappointments.

Take a Closer Look...

Based on what you've learned, reflect on these quotes from Chapter 6:

The supreme happiness of life is the conviction that we are loved.—VICTOR HUGO

_____

_____

_____

_____

_____

No man was ever so deceived by another as by himself.
—FULKE GREVILLE

_____

_____

_____

_____

_____

Study Scriptures: *2 Peter 1:1, 2 Corinthians 5:21, Genesis 3:8-10, Hebrews 9:22, Leviticus 17:11, Hebrews 10:4, Genesis 3:15, Colossians 1:19-20, Ephesians 2:13, Hebrews 9:11-15, Romans 3:25, 2 Corinthians 2:11, Ephesians 4:24, Psalm 11:7, Psalm 5:8, Isaiah 40:3-4, Psalm 85:13, John 14:6, 1 John 1:9, Job 35:2, 36:3*

WORKBOOK CHAPTER SEVEN

The Free Gift

1. This chapter opened with the question: *Have you ever received a gift that was hard to receive?* Yes _____ No _____ Explain your feelings about that:

   _____

   _____

   _____

   _____

   _____

2. Now, in comparison, do you find it hard to receive the gift of forgiveness? Yes _____ No _____ Why or why not?

   _____

   _____

   _____

   _____

   _____

TRUTH

The free gift is not like the offense.

3. If you were to show favor to someone, write down a few
   words describing what that would look like:

   _____

   _____

   _____

   _____

4. We've all sinned, yet the Bible says we've all received
   favor from God. Looking at the words you wrote in
   the last question, do they describe your understanding of what you've received from God through salvation?
   Yes _____ No _____ What's the difference?

   _____

   _____

   _____

   _____

   _____

5. It's a shame to think people might be more excited about
   receiving a free car than they would about receiving salvation and eternal life. I'd like to think people who truly
   understand the magnitude of their free gift of righteousness in Christ would say, "*Oh, happy day!*" Why do you

think people (or yourself) lack enthusiasm for what they've received in Christ?

_____

_____

_____

_____

_____

TRUTH

Regardless of your past, you were made pure and holy and righteous in His sight the moment you confessed and believed upon Jesus Christ as your Savior.

Take a Closer Look...

Based on what you've learned, reflect on these quotes from Chapter 7:

God's gifts put man's best dreams to shame.—ELIZABETH BARRET BROWNING

_____

_____

_____

_____

_____

You can give without loving, but you can never love without giving.—VICTOR HUGO

_____

_____

_____

_____

_____

_____

Study Scriptures: *John 3:16, Romans 5:12, Psalm 51:13, Romans 5:15-17, Luke 1:28-30, Romans 3:23, Hebrews 4:15, Ephesians 6:24, Ephesians 1:6, Titus 3:4-5, Ephesians 2:4-6, 1 Corinthians 6:11, Colossians 1:12, Hebrews 9:12-15*

WORKBOOK CHAPTER EIGHT

Qualified and Convinced

1. Righteousness is right-standing with God, including the ability to stand before Him without guilt or inferiority as if we had never sinned. If you are a believer, the Bible says you are the righteousness of God in Christ. Does the definition of righteousness describe your view of your relationship with God? Explain:

   _____

   _____

   _____

   _____

   _____

2. Jesus had to fulfill the "righteous requirement" of the law so we could be made right with God. Therefore, it's necessary for us to understand this truth: God accounted righteousness to Abraham because he did what?

_____

_____

_____

_____

_____

3. The Bible says Abraham *believed* God. Is that an important factor in our Christian walk also? Why or why not?

_____

_____

_____

_____

_____

_____

TRUTH

To believe: This is all God asked of Abraham, and it's all He ever asks of us.

4. The answer to Question #2 is: *believe.* And yes, it is very important to our Christian walk. To have faith, you must believe. The problem with many Christians is they are not fully convinced of what God's Word says because it doesn't line up with the way they think or view themselves. Is this perhaps some of your problem? If so, how?

_____

_____

_____

_____

_____

5. The Bible says the righteousness given to Abraham was imputed (imparted or given) to all who believe, and it was given to us by God's declaration the moment we were born-again. So is it true? Can you trust what the Bible says? Explain:

_____

_____

_____

_____

_____

Take a Closer Look...

Based on what you've learned, reflect on these quotes from Chapter 8:

To forgive is to set a prisoner free, and then discover the prisoner was you. —LEWIS B. SMEDES

_____

_____

_____

_____

_____

Nothing is more wretched than the mind of a man conscious of guilt.—MACCIUS PLAUTUS

_____

_____

_____

_____

_____

Study Scriptures: *Romans 3:21-24, Romans 8:29-30, Ephesians 2:4-6, Colossians 2:12-14, Romans 10:11, Ephesians 4:7, Romans 8:2-4, 2 Corinthians 5:21, Genesis 15:5-6, Hebrews 6:13-18, Romans 4:20-25, Isaiah 42:6, Romans 10:9-10*

WORKBOOK CHAPTER NINE

Misunderstood Revelation

1. Guilt and condemnation are not God's intentions for the
   believer. However, Paul said learning God's commandments was hard. He desired to learn but the more he did,
   the more overwhelmed he felt with the extent of sin in his
   life. Can you relate? Explain:

   _____

   _____

   _____

   _____

   _____

   _____

TRUTH

**Once a decree has been made by the King,
it cannot be changed.**

---

2. Think about our definitions: Conviction is generally a gentle pull on the inside tugging us to make some changes in our life. Condemnation, on the other hand, is an ugly, harsh voice that causes us to feel like a failure when we recognize sin in our life. Which one has dominated you, and why?

   _____

   _____

   _____

   _____

   _____

3. Can you see how deceptive Satan can be? If he can convince someone they are just a sinner saved by grace, then he has robbed them of the truth regarding their righteousness. Have you ever heard someone say, "I'm just a sinner saved by grace"? Or better yet, have you ever said (or thought) that? Explain:

   _____

   _____

   _____

   _____

   _____

4. Naturally speaking, we've been raised since birth to give attention to our five senses: hearing, seeing, smelling, taste, and touch. After salvation, our spirit awakens with new life and we now have the ability (and responsibility) to develop

discernment of spiritual things. Do you find this hard?
Yes _____ No _____ What role should your natural senses
play in comparison to your spiritual senses?

_____

_____

_____

_____

_____

Take a Closer Look...

Based on what you've learned, reflect on these quotes from
Chapter 9:

*What use is revelation or religion if it doesn't change
anything?*—BAKIR BASHIR

_____

_____

_____

_____

_____

The spiritual is parent of the practical.—THOMAS CARLYLE

_____

_____

_____

_____

_____

_____

Study Scriptures: *Daniel 6, Ephesians 2:8-9, Philippians 1:6, Romans 8:1, Hebrews 5:12, Ephesians 1:7, 1 John 1:9, Hosea 4:6, Romans 7:9-13, Romans 5:18, 1 Corinthians 2:14, 2 Corinthians 5:17, Hebrews 5:13-14, 2 Timothy 2:15, Proverbs 3:5-6, Matthew 6:33*

WORKBOOK CHAPTER TEN

Resisting Condemnation

1. While at a conference, a minister challenged us with this thought: For every year of your life, you should be able to quote one scripture... *accurately.* I remember thinking "Wow... Is that possible?" But, of course it is. If we are serious about having a closer relationship with God, then one of the best things to do is spend time in His Word. The more we know God's Word, the less likely we are to carry around unnecessary guilt and condemnation. So, put yourself to the test. How many scriptures can you quote (accurately)? Try listing a few:

   _____

   _____

   _____

   _____

   _____

   _____

2. If we don't know God's Word says we are forgiven each time we confess, then it is only natural to pick up ugly feelings of guilt and condemnation (again). We grow as we gain knowledge. Before now, what was your understanding of God's forgiveness?

_____

_____

_____

_____

_____

_____

TRUTH

**We need to understand righteousness
is never based on our feelings.**

3. The devil brought sin into this world and condemnation is part of his package. God speaks to us regarding our sin in the form of conviction. How have you allowed condemnation to rest on your shoulders? Explain:

_____

_____

_____

_____

_____

4. Many times we are unsure if we're feeling condemnation or conviction. This is because we give our feelings too much say in the matter. *"There is no condemnation for those... who do not walk according to the flesh (feelings)."* There IS condemnation for those who do. Have you allowed your feelings to have too much say? If yes, then how?

    _____

    _____

    _____

    _____

    _____

    _____

5. God's Word never changes. Our feelings, however, change constantly. If our righteousness was based on how we felt, then very rarely would we have right-standing with God. But our righteousness is *not* based on how we feel—it is based solely on the Word of God. Which one will you believe more, and why?

    _____

    _____

    _____

    _____

    _____

    _____

Take a Closer Look...

Based on what you've learned, reflect on these quotes from Chapter 10:

Compassion will cure more sins than condemnation.

—HENRY WARD BEECHER

_____

_____

_____

_____

_____

Guilt is perhaps the most painful companion to death.

—COCO CHANEL

_____

_____

_____

_____

_____

Study Scriptures: *1 Thessalonians 4:17, Galatians 5:16-17, Romans 7:15, Galatians 5:22-23, Romans 5:18, Romans 8:1, John 3:18, Romans 7:24-25, Romans 7:9-10, John 4:24, Romans 8:5-6*

WORKBOOK CHAPTER ELEVEN

Engrafted

1. Our mind, will, and emotions, are often targeted by Satan to keep us feeling guilty and ashamed. Knowing this, God gave us His Word as a rescue from the lies of Satan and in order to bring healing through the process of engrafting. With an understanding of Jesus' wounds, describe how God's Word has brought healing to your "wounds":

   _____

   _____

   _____

   _____

   _____

   _____

2. I wish we could learn all we need to know by simply observing others. But sadly, we live in a world where confidence in identity is not the norm. Take a minute and think about

the relationships in your life. Are the people closest to you confident in their identity in Christ? Why or why not?

_____

_____

_____

_____

_____

3. The instruction Jesus gave the woman caught in adultery was "Go and sin no more." This is the same instruction He is still giving to all believers. If this is a new thought for you, list some of the instructions you assumed were more important to Jesus:

_____

_____

_____

_____

_____

If not, how have these relationships shaped what you believe?

_____

_____

_____

_____

_____

TRUTH

The best place to discover who you are in Christ is by His example and as described in His Word.

Take a Closer Look...

Based on what you've learned, reflect on these quotes from Chapter 11:

A man finds his identity by identifying.—ROBERT TERWILLIGER

_____

_____

_____

_____

Forgiveness is the fragrance that the flower leaves on the heel of the one who crushed it.—MARK TWAIN

_____

_____

_____

_____

Study Scriptures: *2 Corinthians 5:21, James 1:21, Hebrews 4:12, Psalm 109:21-22, Philippians 1:11, Isaiah 53:4-5, Romans 12:2, John 8:2-11, 1 Corinthians 2:16*

WORKBOOK CHAPTER TWELVE

Performance Not Required

1. Every person with a job gets paid for his or her work, but righteousness isn't a payment. You can work all you want, but it is still a gift that can never be earned. Have you had the mentality that good works will eventually make you righteous? Yes _____ No _____ Is righteousness something you have been working towards? If so, in what way?

   _____

   _____

   _____

   _____

   _____

   _____

2. The Bible says the Gentiles received right-standing with God simply because they believed. But God's chosen people, Israel, who were very religious-minded, assumed they

would receive right-standing with God because of their good deeds. Yet the Bible says they were never declared righteous. Why do certain mindsets never change?

_____

_____

_____

_____

_____

_____

TRUTH

Although it is important to live right and do our best not to sin, those things in and of themselves will not make you any more righteous than you already are.

3. Hopefully, we understand salvation is a free gift. We received it by faith when we confessed Jesus as Lord. "...*no matter who we are or what we have done*" (Romans 3:20,22). Why is righteousness any different?

_____

_____

_____

_____

_____

_____

_____

4. It is important to live what we claim. Therefore, living for God, attending church, and doing good toward others, are definitely part of a Christian's life. How can you follow God's Word without falling into the trap of feeling you need to earn God's approval?

_____

_____

_____

_____

_____

_____

Take a Closer Look...

Based on what you've learned, reflect on these quotes from Chapter 12:

The wheel's spinning, but the hamster's dead.—AUTHOR UNKNOWN

_____

_____

_____

_____

_____

_____

My salvation was a free gift. I didn't have to work for it and it's better than any gold medal I've ever won.—BETTY CUTHBERT (4-TIME OLYMPIC CHAMPION)

_____

_____

_____

_____

_____

Study Scriptures: *Isaiah 64:5, Romans 10:10, Romans 4:1-13, Romans 9:30-32, Romans 10:3-4, Ephesians 2:8-9, Galatians 2:21, Romans 3:20-26, Isaiah 60:10, 1 John 1:5-10, Titus 3:4-5, Isaiah 54:17*

Mirror, Mirror

1. The Bible speaks a lot about the *"glory of the Lord."* Describe what you think His glory looks like:

   _____

   _____

   _____

   _____

   _____

2. According to 2 Corinthians 3:18, when you look in your mirror you are literally looking at the *"glory of the Lord."* How does your description of God's glory in the previous question apply to you? Is it the same or different?

   _____

   _____

   _____

   _____

   _____

TRUTH

Before you can ever truly reflect Christ toward others, you must first see Christ in you.

3. Could you relate to the story of the trashcan? Maybe you've wished you could change, but didn't fully realize you can! God wants you to be transformed so He can use you to reflect His glory to others. If you've desired to be a *"vessel for honor, sanctified and useful for the Master,"* what do you think God is looking for?

    _____

    _____

    _____

    _____

    _____

4. People often shy away from any type of ministry to others simply because they've lost sight of their own value. If you saw a dirty, crumpled, $100 bill lying on the ground, would you ignore it? Step on it? Kick it to the curb? Explain why not, and describe how this applies to the way God sees you:

    _____

    _____

    _____

_____

_____

_____

Take a Closer Look...

Based on what you've learned, reflect on these quotes from Chapter 13:

There are two ways of spreading light: to be the candle or the mirror that reflects it.—EDITH WHARTON

_____

_____

_____

_____

_____

The face is the mirror of the mind, and eyes without speaking confess the secrets of the heart.—ST. JEROME

_____

_____

_____

_____

_____

Study Scriptures: *2 Corinthians 3:18, Colossians 3:10-17, 2 Timothy 2:20-21*

WORKBOOK CHAPTER FOURTEEN

Awakening

1. At the beginning of this book, I challenged you to evaluate what you believe. Has God's Word regarding righteousness, and your new (or refreshed) understanding of it changed the way you believe now? Yes or no, explain:

_____

_____

_____

_____

_____

TRUTH

Every human being has an inner person that needs to be awakened, regardless of what we can see on the outside.

---

2. Do you really want to be like a wave of the sea, changing with every emotion? Yes _____ No _____ God actually designed us to be stable—inside and out. Trials will come and go, but you and I can remain constant based on our belief system regardless of outside influences. But it's the inside influences (our belief system) that need anchoring. So how can you get solid in what you believe?

   _____

   _____

   _____

   _____

   _____

   _____

   _____

3. To have total salvation means to be whole, entire, full-blown, full-scale, undisputed, unlimited, and thorough. If we're not there yet, this is our goal. Write down a few adjectives that describe your salvation up to this point:

   _____

   _____

   _____

   _____

   _____

   _____

   _____

4. Now compare your descriptions with the definition above of total salvation. What are the differences or likenesses?

_____

_____

_____

_____

_____

_____

_____

_____

Take a Closer Look...

Based on what you've learned, reflect on these quotes from Chapter 14:

A single event can awaken a stranger within us totally unknown to us. To live is to be slowly born.—ANTOINE DE SAINT-EXUPERY

_____

_____

_____

_____

_____

_____

_____

Every issue, belief, attitude, or assumption is precisely the issue that stands between you and your relationships; and between you and yourself.—AUTHOR UNKNOWN

_____

_____

_____

_____

_____

_____

Study Scriptures: *1 Corinthians 15:34, 2 Corinthians 5:17, Romans 13:11, Colossians 3:17, Matthew 5:16, Proverbs 12:28, John 11:9-10, 1 Peter 1:3-9, Philippians 1:21, Romans 14:9, James 1:6-8, Romans 14:217-23, 2 Corinthians 12:2-5, 2 Timothy 2:13*

WORKBOOK CHAPTER FIFTEEN

Living Out Our Righteousness

1. Regardless of where a person was raised or from what family they came from, almost everyone struggles with the *speaking* side of faith. And for the most part, the enemy has done a good job at making believers feel silly or prideful when they even try. So how about you? Describe your experience, or understanding, of the speaking part of faith:

   _____

   _____

   _____

   _____

   _____

   _____

2. Build your own formula: Fill in the blanks with how your faith has operated thus far.

   _____ part(s) say = _____ part(s) belief

So what now?

3. One thing is certain: You have been made the righteousness of God in Christ, but your flesh is still tempted to sin. None of us are perfect. And God knows this. He also knows sin separates us from Him so He provided a way for us to stay in right relationship with Him through prayer and repentance. Think about the times you asked God for forgiveness. According to His Word, regardless of what it was you had done, were you forgiven and re-established in righteousness? And how do you know?

    _____

    _____

    _____

    _____

    _____

    _____

    _____

4. You aren't working towards righteousness, but you do have to guard and protect your *knowledge* of it. The devil is a liar and he finds great joy in sitting on your shoulder whispering contradictions in your ear. Do you try to fight back with the knowledge of who you are in Christ? Or do you just listen (and even entertain) the voice of condemnation? Explain (and if necessary, describe changes you need to make):

_____

_____

_____

_____

_____

_____

_____

5. Condemnation can have deep roots that have to be pulled up. But afterward, don't leave the ground barren. Instead, replant with seeds of righteousness! You do this by saying what God has already said of you: *"I am the righteousness of God in Christ."*

_____

_____

_____

_____

_____

_____

(Don't stop! Say it again and again and again—until you believe it!)

6. Spiritual maturity isn't based on how long you've been saved; it's based on your application of God's Word. If faith is like a muscle, then we need to exercise it. We need to push away all doubts, insecurities, and lies by

confessing the truth of God's Word. So what can you begin to do right now on a daily basis to build your faith?

_____

_____

_____

_____

_____

Hopefully, you have gained some new knowledge about who you are in Christ. Or maybe you've been reminded of things you already knew. Either way, it's time to use your knowledge and apply it!

One final question:

7. Have you ever taken a foreign language class? Yes _____ No _____ If yes, what would happen if you never used what you learned?

_____

_____

_____

_____

_____

Remember, knowledge of God's Word is no different.

You are who God says you are. In fact, I am quite confident… you are the righteousness of God in Christ!

Take a Closer Look...

Based on what you've learned, reflect on these quotes from Chapter 15:

A little knowledge that acts is worth infinitely more than much knowledge that is idle. —KAHILL GIBRAN

_____

_____

_____

_____

_____

All the art of living lies in a fine mingling of letting go and holding on. —HAVELOCK ELLIS

_____

_____

_____

_____

_____

Study Scriptures: *Philippians 3:1, 2 Corinthians 5:21, Romans 8:1, 2 Corinthians 4:13, Hebrews 11:1-34, Mark 11:22-23, Romans 4:18, 2 Corinthians 5:7, Matthew 12:34, 1 John 1:9, Isaiah 43:25, 1 Timothy 6:11-12, Jeremiah 29:11, Psalm 92:12, James 1:22-25, John 10:10, Philippians 3:9-14*

Notes

Chapter Three

1. San Souci, Robert D. *Mulan.* [Video] Prod. Walt Disney Pictures, 1998.

2. Jones, Beth. *Getting a Grip on the Basics.* Tulsa, OK: Harrison House, Inc., 1994.

Chapter Four

1. Where Grace Abounds, www.wheregraceabounds.org

Chapter Six

1. Burlingame, Michael. *For the People.* Available at: http://www.abrahamlincolnassociation.org/Newsletters/1-1.pdf (accessed November 13, 2012).

Chapter Seven

1. *Webster's Encyclopedia Unabridged Dictionary of the English Language,* s.v. *favor.*

2. Oldenburg, Ann. *$7M Car Giveaway Stuns TV Audience.* Available at: http://usatoday30.usatoday.com/life/

people/2004-09-13-oprah-cars_x.htm (accessed November 13, 2012).

Chapter Eight

1. *Vine's Expository Dictionary of New Testament Words*, s.v. *justification*.

Chapter Nine

1. Kenyon, E.W. *New Creation Realities*. Kenyon's Gospel Publishing Society, Inc., 2000.

Chapter Fourteen

1. http://www.oliversacks.com/about-the-author/biography (accessed November 13, 2012).

Chapter Fifteen

1. *Webster's Encyclopedia Unabridged Dictionary of the English Language*, s.v. *faith*.

2. *Webster's Encyclopedia Unabridged Dictionary of the English Language*, s.v. *perception*.

3. Brazee, Mark. *365 Days of Healing*. Harrison House, 1999, 2003, 2006.

About the Author

Daphne Delay is a writer who loves Jesus because He loved her first. Her favorite topic is righteousness (yep, that big-sounding Bible word) and her goal is to make it easy-to-grasp and understand.

She is the author of *Facing the Mirror*, *Facing the Enemy*, *Facing God*, and a 365-day devotional, *Facing the Wall*. Her books and workbooks are used in prisons and rehab centers helping people learn how to receive God's love and forgiveness, recognize and overcome the lies of the enemy, and walk in their identity in Christ.

Daphne travels and speaks frequently. She and her husband Tod have been the senior pastors at Transformation Church in Seminole, Texas, since 1999. They have three grown, married children (all in the ministry also) and several adorable grandkids.

Contact Daphne

Daphne speaks frequently on the topic of righteousness. She can share a keynote, half-day, full-day, or retreat version of this content, depending on your needs. For more information, or to subscribe to her blog, podcast, and other resources, please visit her website at *daphnedelay.com*.

You can also connect with Daphne here:

Instagram: *instagram.com/daphnedelay*
Facebook: *facebook.com/daphnedelayMM*
Twitter: *twitter.com/daphnedelay*

You can also write to:

Mirror Ministries
PO Box 1418
Seminole, TX 79360

PRAYER OF SALVATION

God loves you—no matter who you are, no matter what your past. God loves you so much that he gave his one and only begotten Son for you. The Bible tells us that ". . . whoever believes in him shall not perish but have eternal life" (John 3:16 NIV). Jesus laid down His life and rose again so that we could spend eternity with Him and experience His absolute best on earth. If you would like to receive Jesus into your life, say the following prayer out loud and mean it in your heart.

Heavenly Father, I come to you admitting that I am a sinner. Right now, I choose to turn away from sin, and I ask you to cleanse me of all unrighteousness. I believe that Your son, Jesus, died on the cross to take away my sins. I also believe that he rose again from the dead so that I might be forgiven of my sins and made righteous through faith in him. I call upon the name of Jesus Christ to be the Savior and Lord of my life. Jesus, I choose to follow You and ask You that You fill me with the power of the Holy Spirit. I declare that right now I am a child of God. I am free from sin and full of the righteousness of God. I am saved in Jesus' name. Amen.

If you prayed this prayer to receive Jesus Christ as your Savior for the first time, please contact us by writing to us.

www.harrisonhouse.com
Harrison House
PO Box 310
Shippensburg, PA 17257

What began as an encounter with God in front of a mirror launched a mandate. And Mirror Ministries with Daphne Delay was born over 20 years ago.

Daphne's books and workbooks are used in prisons to help minister truths to inmates who not only live in literal prisons but are often imprisoned in the guilt and condemnation of their choices. Although never having been in prison herself, Daphne's heart broke at the thought of men and women living in a double prison, not knowing the truth of how God sees them and the forgiveness and righteousness He offers us in Christ.

Learn more at
daphnedelay.com

In 2018, God opened a big door for my books to get into prisons. I received a letter from a woman who had been incarcerated for over 12 years. She had been given a copy of *Facing the Mirror* by a friend of mine in prison ministry. She said that of all the material she had read, this book helped her find forgiveness and hope. I was then invited to go into the prison with their team, where I got to meet inmates and take cases of books to give away. Not only was my heart deeply touched by this encounter, but letters began to pour in from inmates requesting books.

THE MISSION WAS BIRTHED: Give 10,000 books to inmates.

God wants people to be free. Those incarcerated didn't receive the right tools before they ended up on a road God never intended for any of us to travel. This ministry may not be able to free them outwardly, but through the message of righteousness, we can help free them inwardly.

INMATE TESTIMONIES:

"Your book has taken my mind and spirit to another level. Because of your book, I now understand God's love, purpose, and grace. I also understand my place in His Kingdom. I am filled with so much joy, love, and determination to serve my God!" —*Delvin*

"After I read *Facing the Mirror*, I actually looked at myself in the mirror and saw a new reflection—my inner person. This study has made me aware of the devil's schemes and showed me how to lean on Jesus to help me through doubts, guilt, and condemnation. I'm grateful to know that God has forgiven me for my past sins and that I have a new beginning." —*Tom*

"I want to personally thank you for writing these books and giving people like me an opportunity to read them. *Facing the Mirror* truly made me look deeper into myself and into my relationship with God." —*Brittany*

"*Facing the Mirror* has helped me grow spiritually in a great and positive way. Every chapter taught me something or taught me a new, proper way of thinking about something. Especially how to not let the devil make me believe that my past could keep me from what God has promised true believers. My faith is increased!" —*Benjamin*

"Not only were these great books, but I got a chance to find our who I was, who I am now, and who God wants me to be. One thing I'll never forget is that the mirror never lies and for me that was something big because I wasn't ready but I've learned to accept God's love, so thank you again for your books." —*Cornelio*

"These studies have been life changing. I just love the way Daphne put them together. Her wording and perspective helped me so much!" —*Sandy*

"I want to say thank you so much for sharing these truths with me as I strengthen my walk with Father God. I'm grateful to learn who I am and I plan on taking my rightful place as a kingdom-minded child of God!" —*Elkeshius*

"Thank you Daphne. Your knowledge of the Spirit made me look in the mirror. I grew confident that there is no condemnation to those who are in Christ!" —*Robert*

"I have to say thank you for giving me what I feel like is a sort of guide to my inner spirit and letting me know how close I actually am with God versus what I thought." —*Andrew*

OTHER BOOKS BY DAPHNE DELAY

In this book, Daphne explains in great detail three areas that are imperative for Christians to understand: righteousness, deception, and authority. God's Word has given us specific strategies concerning all three, which equip and prepare us to win behind enemy lines. God never intended believers to live defeated!

This is the story of the man who challenged God— the man God originally called blameless. But was he? Are any of us? What we know for sure is, the Lord used the story of Job to illustrate His never-ending mercy and compassion to cover our sins and teach us His ways.

In this 365-day devotional, Daphne expounds God's Word with insight and revelation to help guide you. The Bible says, "There's a private place reserved for the lovers of god, where they sit near him and receive the revelation-secrets of his promises" (Psalm 25:14, TPT).

From

Trina Hankins

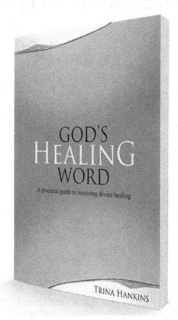

Read the testimony of how Trina was healed by God of an inoperable brain tumor.

God's Healing Word contains Trina's testimony, many other powerful testimonies of people who were healed by the power of God, practical teaching designed to help you receive your healing, scriptures and confessions on healing that will strengthen your faith, and a CD with healing scriptures being read by Rev. Mark Hankins.

Purchase your copy wherever books are sold

From

Dr. Pat Harrison

Now more than ever the body of Christ must mature in the ways of the Spirit to fulfill God's plan for His kingdom as the clock ticks steadily toward the return of Jesus Christ. The only way we will fulfill the Great Commission Jesus left us is to have both the indwelling presence of the Holy Spirit and His power fully operating in our lives. The problem is most believers don't know the difference between the two or how to walk in the fullness of all God has called us to do. In some ways, we've had things backwards and short-circuited God's best.

In *Overflowing with the Holy Spirit*, author Pat Harrison teaches about the dual role of the Holy Spirit in your life—to establish you first in the indwelling and then in the outpouring. The working of the Holy Spirit within matures you in holiness and oneness with Jesus. Then the outpouring comes upon you with power, ability, efficiency, and might to bless others. Understanding the two intertwined facets will help you walk in the *fullness of both*—until you're *overflowing with the Spirit in everyday life*.

Purchase your copy wherever books are sold

YOUR HOUSE OF
FAITH

Sign up for **FREE** Subscription to the
Harrison House digital magazine, and get
excellent content delivered directly to your inbox!

harrisonhouse.com/signup

Sign-up for Messages that Equip You to Walk in the Abundant Life

• Receive biblically-sound and Spirit-filled encouragement to focus on and maintain your faith
• Grow in faith through biblical teachings, prayers, and other spiritual insights
• Connect with a community of believers who share your values and beliefs

Experience Fresh Teachings and Inspiration to Build Your Faith

• Deepen your understanding of God's purpose for your life
• Stay connected and inspired on your faith journey
• Learn how to grow spiritually in your walk with God